ADHD WOMEN: THE A-Z GUIDE FOR COPING AND THRIVING

MANAGE YOUR ADULT ADHD WITH PROVEN CBT TECHNIQUES, BUILD BETTER HABITS, IMPROVE EXECUTIVE FUNCTIONING AND EMOTIONAL WELL-BEING

WILDA HALE

CONTENTS

MEDICAL DISCLAIMER

INTRODUCTION

At 30 years old, I found out that I have ADHD. In the months leading up to this finding, I started out on what you might call a soul-searching path, as I felt so astonished and disappointed by my lack of achievement in life. Despite constantly improving on a personal level and being a hard worker in my professional life, I hadn't been able to make the strides that I've always known I was capable of. Also, I knew deep down that I was smart enough, despite all the external evidence indicating otherwise. So what was wrong with me?

A while ago, I accidentally stumbled upon some articles about ADHD. I thought I knew what ADHD was from brief previous readings, but I learned quite quickly that I most definitely didn't. Normally, I wouldn't have been too curious about reading up on the subject, but at that moment, something called me to it. I had never really considered that I could have ADHD because, in my ignorance back then, I thought it was something outwardly obvious. I think that I believed in the old cliché of the annoying kid who couldn't stay still even if their life depended on it, as the representation of ADHD. Or perhaps the cliché belief that anyone with ADHD was extremely talk-ative, constantly overly energetic, and a little bit scattered all the time. Me on the other hand? I'd always considered myself to have pretty standard energy levels, and I was never that extroverted and exceedingly chatty, so there was no chance that I could have it!

After reading more about the symptoms and how they really manifest, I began to feel like someone was telling me stories of my own past and describing with uncanny accuracy how my mind worked:

Countless mental tabs open at all times? Check!

Frequently forgetting what I was saying mid-sentence? Check!

Getting easily bored? Check!

A hot temper? Check!

Fairly clumsy? Check!

Extremely creative brain? Definite check!

The more I read about the topic, the more "checks" added up. I started to have flashbacks: I'd see myself in the first grade at school, always daydreaming and looking out the window. I'd remember how, at every teacher-parent meeting, my teacher would tell my mom that I rarely paid attention in class. I'd recall moments from my classes, struggling to keep the same pace as others when taking notes, only to eventually lose track of what the teacher was saying and then have to ask for my friends' notes to fill in the gaps. Weirdly enough, I did reason-ably well in school, but it wasn't until later that I realized how much harder than others I was working to cope with my lack of attention and to hide my shortcomings.

I also recalled moments from early adulthood where I'd been overwhelmed at work—in basic jobs, where the average person was performing up to par but I, on the other hand, was falling short. As a waitress, I was so overwhelmed by having to juggle between taking orders, checking the kitchen for food orders that were ready, cleaning up tables and checking in with customers. I also worked as a housekeeper during my summers at university, and I remember my supervisor always criticizing me because I'd often do a sloppy job despite trying really hard not to, missing many of the areas that were meant to be cleaned.

These are just two examples out of many, but there were plenty of other jobs I did poorly at, all because I struggled with attention or memorizing certain aspects of the job. And what's worse is that I couldn't understand why.

I felt like a failure. Incapable. Dumb. There were so many basic things that I was so bad at for no apparent reason. I knew that I wasn't stupid, but for some reason the outside didn't reflect my true self and my potential by any means. So then *what was it*? Well, it would be years until I would finally unravel things enough to truly figure it out...

Why I Wrote This Book

In the midst of my journey, a spark ignited in me. I felt compelled to write a book for women with ADHD, inspired by my own struggles and the ways I managed to overcome many of them. Essentially, I wanted to write a book containing all the information and solutions I wish that I'd had years earlier.

I hope these pages will guide you on this often-messy journey, and to remind you that you're not alone. Mental health challenges often leave us feeling isolated, unaware that many others are traversing very similar paths.

Whether you've already been diagnosed or you merely suspect at this point that you may have ADHD, this book will be a compass in your journey.

Moreover, I wanted women to know that life with ADHD isn't just about trying to overcome challenges and managing symptoms but also about recognizing and cultivating the many qualities that come along with ADHD—the wellspring of creativity, curiosity, resilience, energy, empathy, intuition, and humor—just to name a few.

By the end of this book, you'll have a newfound self-awareness that will help you better express what you've been feeling for so long. You'll also learn plenty of practical techniques that will help you navigate ADHD with greater ease.

More specifically, within the pages of this book you'll discover:

- The most common indicators of ADHD in women, as well as some not-so-obvious ones
- How to overcome your ADHD-related negative self-beliefs
- Some conventional and alternative treatment solutions to best manage your ADHD
- Coping strategies to help you navigate executive function challenges
- Behavioral techniques to help you become more organized, productive, and focused
- How to best manage romance, work, and social life as a woman with ADHD
- How to accept your ADHD-related differences

This book will be your roadmap to understanding, managing, and eventually celebrating the unique journey of being a woman with ADHD.

1

ADHD 101

"Living with ADHD is like being locked in a room with 100 televisions and 100 radios all playing. None of them have power buttons, so you can't turn them off, and the door is locked from the outside."
— Sarah Young, American author

*B*efore we dive in, I must state that I realize some of you may already be familiar with the basics of ADHD from previous readings. However, I'd like to cover the basics at the outset here to make sure that everyone reading this book understands what ADHD is all about. That said, if you already know the ABCs of ADHD, feel free to skip ahead to Chapter 2.

What Is ADHD?

ADHD (attention-deficit/hyperactivity disorder) is a common neurodevelopmental condition that primarily affects how our brains manage attention, impulses, and activity levels.

Brains with ADHD work differently than neurotypical ones. In ADHD brains, there's an imbalance in some key neurotransmitters[1], like dopamine and norepinephrine. This leads to the characteristic ADHD symptoms, like trouble with focusing, controlling impulses, and other executive processes such as decision making, planning, or problem solving.

As individuals with ADHD, we deal with a constant stream of thoughts and stimuli that often feel beyond our control. Our minds are constantly active and prone to distraction, making managing daily activities challenging.

Though called "attention deficit," ADHD is not necessarily about having less attention, but rather the struggle to control it effectively. Dr. Edward Hallowell, psychiatrist and author of the book *ADHD 2.0*, created one of the finest analogies depicting the ADHD brain: "The power of a Ferrari engine but with bicycle-strength brakes." This comparison perfectly illustrates the pairing of great potential and mental energy with attention difficulties and impulsivity.

Is It Called ADD or ADHD?

The term ADD (attention deficit disorder) transitioned to ADHD in the *Diagnostic and Statistical Manual of Mental Disorders* (DSM) during the revision from DSM-III to DSM-IV[2]. This change in terminology was made to more accurately encompass the diverse range of symptoms associated with ADHD. However, some people still use the term "ADD" in everyday conversation due to its historical use and perhaps remaining unaware of the name change.

Types of ADHD

According to the American Psychiatric Association, there are three types of ADHD: inattentive, hyperactive-impulsive, and combined.

Predominantly inattentive: Someone with inattentive ADHD (formerly known as ADD) primarily has difficulties sustaining attention, being organized, following through on tasks, and paying attention to details. They may often struggle following detailed instructions, forget what they're talking about mid-sentence, are frequently late to appointments, or have a knack for losing or misplacing things.

Those with inattentive ADHD generally don't display as much hyperactivity or impulsivity. This type of ADHD tends to be more common among females.

Predominantly hyperactive-impulsive: People with this ADHD presentation generally find it difficult to sit still, often interrupt conversations, talk a lot and very fast, act on impulses without considering consequences, and may also struggle to wait their turn. This type is most often diagnosed in children and men.

Combined: Among people with ADHD, the combined presentation is the most common. Those with this type of experience both inattentive and hyperactive-impulsive traits.

It's a Spectrum

An essential aspect to note is the fact that ADHD is a spectrum disorder, meaning that it can vary widely in its presentation, as well as its severity, across different people. There's a lot of variation when it comes to how impairing ADHD is. For some people, it can be profoundly disruptive, affecting almost every aspect of daily life, while others experience milder difficulties.

The spectrum nature of ADHD is also related to the fact that people experience varying degrees of inattentive- and hyperactive-type symptoms.

Moreover, ADHD sometimes coexists with other conditions, like anxiety, depression, mood and eating disorders, or learning disabilities, which can further contribute to the spectrum-like presentation.

Five Common Myths Surrounding ADHD

There are many myths out there about ADHD—from the common "everyone has a little bit of ADHD" to "ADHD is just another invented diagnosis that enables Big Pharma to sell more drugs." I think that it's essential to dismantle some of these common misconceptions surrounding ADHD and shed some light on the facts.

1. "ADHD is just a Big Pharma plot."

To this day, some people out there still think that ADHD is a conspiracy created by pharmaceutical companies to sell medications. We've already clarified in the previous section of this chapter that ADHD is a legitimate neurodevelopmental condition, and while medication can be helpful for many, it truly isn't some grand scheme created by Big Pharma.

2. "We all have a little ADHD."

Eye roll. Big sigh. In a way, I get why some less-informed people would say, "Everyone's a little ADHD," because we all experience the occasional distraction, procrastination, or bout of fidgeting, but this is like saying that a drizzle is the same as a monsoon. ADHD is not just minor distractibility and laziness; it stems from fundamental brain-wiring differences. Those of us with ADHD struggle to be more organized and focused due to these neurodevelopmental differences, despite our best efforts.

3. "ADHD is simply a lack of discipline."

These ones are classic (and cringeworthy!): "If you just tried harder..." or "If you'd only try to be a little bit more organized..." By now, it should be clear that ADHD isn't a matter of lack of discipline and focus—it's a wiring thing. Telling someone with ADHD to try harder is like telling someone with color blindness to distinguish between red and green.

4. "They'll outgrow it."

Nope! ADHD is for life. The belief that ADHD is just a childhood phase that'll eventually be outgrown is all too common. While it may evolve as a person ages or become less pronounced due to treatments and coping techniques, ADHD is going to stick around for the rest of one's life. (Apologies if I'm the one to break it to you!)

5. ADHD = Hyperactivity

It was long believed that only children and adults displaying hyperactive behavior could have ADHD. But, as mentioned in the previous section on ADHD types, some individuals (particularly women) primarily exhibit inattentive behavior. Fortunately, increased awareness in recent years has significantly diminished this stereotype associated with ADHD.

The Not-So-Obvious ADHD Symptoms

"Why did no one know? Why didn't anyone notice sooner?" These are sensible questions to ask, and they're, in fact, fairly common among the many adult women who lived most of their lives without a clue that what they were experiencing was ADHD. Women who lived without the relief of a diagnosis internalized feelings of inadequacy, a sense of failure, and self-blame.

While hyperactivity and inattention are commonly associated with ADHD, there are so many other subtle signs that point to the condition, but they often go unrecognized, being instead attributed to personality or other factors.

Increasing awareness of these less obvious signs is crucial. I've included a list below of 15 symptoms that often fly under the radar, particularly in women:

1. **Frequent boredom.** Our high need for stimulation often makes us prone to restlessness and boredom if we're not constantly engaged.

2. **Daydreaming or mind wandering.** While inattention is a core symptom, it can sometimes manifest in subtler ways, like daydreaming or a continuous flow of distracting thoughts, making it challenging to focus.

3. **Low motivation.** Our executive function[3] difficulties make it hard to stay motivated, especially for monotonous tasks.

4. **Hyperfocus.** As paradoxical as it may sound, since distractibility is a hallmark symptom of ADHD, we can also hyperfocus on activities that really interest us. During those moments, we become deeply absorbed and unable to shift our attention, which frequently leads to losing track of time.

5. Emotional dysregulation. We tend to have intense emotional reactions and mood swings. We're often impulsive, hypersensitive to criticism, and struggle to manage our emotions or control our temper.

6. Rejection sensitivity dysphoria (RSD). RSD is characterized by extreme emotional sensitivity and pain in response to criticism or perceived rejection. For example, even minor signs of disapproval—like a subtle negative comment or disapproving look related to something we've said or done—can trigger intense emotions such as sadness and anxiety. Feelings like this can make us want to avoid social situations altogether.

7. Chronic procrastination. This is one of the most common challenges that ADHD brings, and it doesn't have anything to do with laziness—it stems from difficulties with executive functions. We struggle to start on a task and maintain our focus, which often leads to delaying something until the last moment.

8. Working memory deficits. We often struggle with retaining information, particularly while multitasking or performing complex mental tasks. Issues with working memory can also impact our organizational abilities.

9. Organizational difficulties and forgetfulness. Similar to chronic procrastination, these symptoms result from challenges related to executive functions, like consistent issues with time management, planning, or prioritizing, leading to a sense of overwhelm and a cluttered physical environment. We may frequently misplace items or lose track of tasks.

10. Time blindness. Some of us struggle with accurately estimating the passing of time. We may frequently be late because we underestimate how long getting ready or commuting will actually take us.

11. Sensory sensitivities. We tend to be highly sensitive to noises, strong smells and tastes, bright lights, or textures. For example, we can find the ticking of a clock incredibly distracting, or a particular clothing fabric so uncomfortable that it gets overwhelming. Things like these can negatively impact our comfort and focus.

12. Difficulty with transitions. Switching between tasks or activities is challenging for most of us, leading to stress and resistance.

13. Social difficulties. Our scattered focus can sometimes make reading social cues difficult. Also, our impulsiveness can bring challenges to our conversations and affect our relationships in general, as some of us sometimes may have a tendency to interrupt.

14. Sleep problems. ADHD can make it difficult to fall asleep at night or wake up in the morning. We often struggle with insomnia and irregular sleep patterns.

15. Intense interest shifts. We tend to start new projects and activities with a lot of excitement and motivation, but it doesn't take long until we lose interest and leave them incomplete.

In the following chapters, we'll delve deeper into these symptoms and explore the most effective ways to manage them.

Causes of ADHD

Certain factors—like genetics, environmental factors, or premature birth—can increase the risk of developing ADHD. However, none of these guarantee that someone will have the disorder.

Genetics: There's a strong genetic component to ADHD, as it tends to run in families. So if a blood relative, such as a parent, has ADHD, there's a high chance that you may also have it.

Environmental factors: Early childhood factors may contribute to the development of ADHD. These factors include exposure to toxins during pregnancy, maternal smoking, or substance abuse during pregnancy.

Premature birth: This can bring certain complications, among which may be a higher risk of ADHD. Early birth is believed to affect the normal development of the brain, particularly those areas of the brain related to attention and impulse control.

Coexisting Conditions

It's estimated that about two-thirds of ADHD people also have coexisting conditions, which often complicate the diagnosis and treatment of ADHD due to symptom overlap. This high-lights the importance of being aware of these aspects in order to prevent a potential misdiagnosis and ensure that we get the best approach to our mental health. Moreover, it demonstrates the importance of an assessment by a qualified and experi-enced mental health professional, as well as a tailored treat-ment plan that addresses all coexisting conditions.

Anxiety disorders, like generalized anxiety, panic disorder, or social anxiety, frequently manifest in people with ADHD. It's been observed that women, in particular, are more prone to experiencing high levels of anxiety, worry, and stress.

Depression is another commonly occuring condition alongside ADHD. The multitude of challenges associated with ADHD can contribute to feelings of hopelessness and a persistently low mood.

Bipolar disorder (BD) is characterized by alternating periods of depression and mania. BD and ADHD share many similar symptoms, like impulsivity, irritability, and mood swings. Because of this, some people with ADHD have been misdiagnosed with BD (and vice versa). This overlap can make it difficult to differentiate between the two conditions, particularly during periods of mood instability when one condition's symptoms may overshadow the other's. It's crucial for a clinician to differentiate between the two, as their treatment approaches differ significantly. In addition, stimulant medication, commonly used for ADHD, can trigger or worsen manic episodes in individuals with bipolar disorder.

Eating disorders (such as bulimia, anorexia, and binge eating disorder) are quite common among individuals with ADHD, since impulsivity and emotional dysregulation contribute significantly to these abnormal eating behaviors.

Sometimes, ADHD may coexist with another neurodevelopmental disorder, such as **ASD (autistic spectrum disorder)**. ADHD and ASD share a few common characteristics, like difficulties with social interactions or challenges with attention and focus.

Learning difficulties, such as dyslexia or dyscalculia, are typical in people with ADHD and can often negatively impact academic performance and self-esteem.

Sleep disorders are quite common among individuals with ADHD, and include difficulties with falling asleep, staying asleep, or having a restful sleep. ADHD and sleep disorders have a bidirectional relationship, with each condition amplifying the symptoms of the other. Sleep difficulties often worsen ADHD symptoms, leading to problems with focus, attention, impulsivity, disruptions in executive functions like planning, organization, and time management, as well as increased hyperactivity. On the other hand, ADHD affects sleep in various ways, as a restless mind, hyperactivity, impulsivity, and shifted sleep patterns can hinder falling asleep and staying asleep. On top of that, certain medications used for ADHD, like stimulants, can interfere with sleep.

Borderline personality disorder (BPD) and ADHD have some overlapping symptoms, like emotional instability and impulsive behavior, and these occasionally coexist in some people.

Obsessive-compulsive disorder (OCD) can sometimes coexist with ADHD, and the two can amplify each other's symptoms. ADHD-related impulsivity and distractibility can heighten OCD traits. Conversely, OCD symptoms, like repetitive behaviors and intrusive thoughts, can interfere with and disrupt focus and attention.

Post-traumatic stress disorder (PTSD). Traumatic experiences can lead to PTSD and ADHD-like symptoms, as trauma can result in difficulties with focus and attention. Moreover, the emotional distress and hypervigilance associated with PTSD can increasingly disrupt executive functions. These overlapping symptoms can make an accurate diagnosis difficult.

Addiction to various substances. Many people with ADHD have a higher risk of developing addiction to various substances, as these can often be used as a way to cope with the challenges and emotional difficulties of ADHD.

Women & ADHD

According to studies, over 50% of adult women with ADHD are undiagnosed. And for those who *do* receive a diagnosis, it often occurs in their late 30s or early 40s. [4] [5] Sadly, for most—if not all—of their lives, many women remain unaware of their ADHD, incorrectly attributing its symptoms to their personality traits and personal shortcomings.

Several factors contribute to the high prevalence of undiagnosed ADHD in women. A significant one is the limited research on female-specific ADHD symptoms. For decades, studies have been conducted primarily on males, and the diagnostic criteria have been based on the observations from these studies. However, ADHD symptoms in women often manifest quite differently than in men, and therefore don't align with the standard criteria. This historical bias has led to the misconception that ADHD predominantly affects males.

Typically, men display more externalized behaviors, such as hyperactivity and impulsivity, while women most frequently present more subtle and internalized symptoms, such as inattention, emotional dysregulation, and daydreaming. The fact that female ADHD symptoms don't align with the conventional understanding and stereotypical image of ADHD has resulted in these symptoms being largely overlooked. Moreover, these differences have often led to misinterpretations, with the symptoms frequently being mistaken for mood disorders or anxiety.

Also, despite recent progress in normalizing discussions around mental health, a stigma still remains. This can often discourage many from seeking evaluation and treatment in the first place.

Another contributing factor to the low percentage of ADHD diagnoses among females is the fact that many girls and women develop effective coping mechanisms to compensate for their challenges. These strategies make their ADHD less visible, allowing them to fly under the radar. The well-practiced coping mechanisms often also result in women downplaying their symptoms during assessments, making it challenging even for healthcare professionals to identify their ADHD.

Additionally, research[6] has revealed that many women simultaneously have coexisting conditions, such as anxiety, depression, autism spectrum disorder, personality disorders, mood disorders, and eating disorders. These often overshadow and mask the presence of ADHD, leading to misdiagnoses and inadequate treatment.

Furthermore, society doesn't make things easy for women with ADHD. Societal expectations placed upon females include behaviors such as attentiveness, organization, and self-control. When we struggle in these areas, our difficulties are often attributed to immaturity or personal shortcomings.

Fortunately, mental health specialists have come to better understand these factors in recent years. Although there's still a long way to go, they seem to be on the right track when it comes to raising awareness and advocating for accurate diagnosis and treatment for women. The medical community has acknowledged these issues, and has implemented initiatives aimed at enhancing the understanding of female-specific ADHD symptoms, developing gender-specific diagnostic criteria, and raising awareness among healthcare professionals, teachers, and parents to ensure that girls and women with ADHD receive the support that they need.

Women's Hormones and ADHD

Hormones play an essential role in how ADHD manifests in women. Key hormonal phases include menstrual cycles, pregnancy, postpartum, and the use of hormonal birth control. The fluctuations of estrogen and progesterone during these times impact serotonin and dopamine levels, affecting mood, impulsivity, and overall functioning of women with ADHD. Careful monitoring of individual reactions to hormonal shifts allows women to better understand and manage their mental health.

Menstrual cycle: Fluctuations in estrogen and progesterone levels during the menstrual cycle can significantly impact a woman's ADHD. Many women notice that symptoms such as inattention and impulsivity worsen during certain phases of their menstrual cycle, particularly in the premenstrual phase.

Pregnancy: Some women experience improvements in their ADHD symptoms during pregnancy and this is believed to occur due to the rise of estrogen levels, which can have a stabilizing effect on neurotransmitters. In some instances, however, the stressors and demands of pregnancy can negatively affect ADHD women, making some symptoms more pronounced.

Postpartum: Following pregnancy, the postpartum period involves a rapid drop in estrogen and progesterone, and this hormonal shift leads to an increased risk of depression and anxiety. Also, the demands of caring for a newborn may be overwhelming for many women living with ADHD.

Hormonal birth control: Some women with ADHD have reported changes in their symptoms while using hormonal birth control methods. The effects of hormonal birth control on ADHD however are mixed—while some women experience relief of symptoms, others report worsening. Therefore, each woman must monitor how hormonal birth control affects her ADHD symptoms.

KEY TAKEAWAYS:

1. ADHD is a neurodevelopmental disorder characterized by difficulties with attention, impulse control, and activity levels.

2. ADD is a term that's no longer used. It transitioned into ADHD to better encompass the condition's diverse symptoms.

3. There are three types of ADHD: inattentive, hyperactive-impulsive, and combined.

4. ADHD is a spectrum disorder with varying levels of severity. It manifests in individuals differently, often coexisting with other conditions.

5. Beyond hyperactivity and inattention, ADHD presents many subtle symptoms, such as emotional dysregulation, chronic procrastination, low motivation, frequent boredom, working memory deficits, organizational difficulties, time blindness, sensory sensitivities, transition difficulties, social challenges, sleep problems, and intense interest shifts.

6. The leading causes of ADHD are genetics, environmental factors, and premature birth.

7. ADHD often coexists with various conditions, including mood disorders, addiction, personality disorders, or learning disabilities.

8. Many adult women remain undiagnosed until their late 30s or 40s due to factors such as limited research on female-specific symptoms, gender bias, or the use of coping mechanisms that tend to hide symptoms.

9. Hormonal fluctuations that occur due to the menstrual cycle, pregnancy, postpartum, or hormonal birth control use can affect ADHD symptoms in women, influencing mood, impulsivity, and overall functioning. Monitoring these shifts can help women better manage their ADHD.

2

CONVENTIONAL & ALTERNATIVE SOLUTIONS FOR ADHD

"You may encounter many defeats, but you must not be defeated. In fact, it may be necessary to encounter the defeats so you can know who you are, what you can rise from, and how you can come out of it."
— Maya Angelou, American memoirist and poet

The journey to finding the right treatment for ADHD can feel like wandering through a never-ending maze. There are so many options, each promising relief, clarity, and focus. How do we choose what's best for us?

It's easy to feel overwhelmed when combing through the large variety of treatment options for ADHD. I definitely felt that way early into my journey, googling late into the night about Adderall and psychotherapy, as well as weighing the pros and cons of alternative and conventional medicine. It's a lot to figure out. So in order to help you understand your options, in the following pages, we'll explore the wide range of treatment approaches for ADHD, including:

- Conventional medicine
- Alternative treatments
- Therapy
- Dietary changes
- Exercise
- Sleep hygiene

This chapter will empower you to make informed decisions about what's right for YOU. When dealing with ADHD, there's no such thing as a one-size-fits-all solution. Certain therapies, lifestyle changes, and medications will be game changers, while some will have little to no effect. Allow yourself the time to test different approaches and tweak things along the way, because discovering the winning formula of what works best for you takes patience and perseverance. So remember to be compassionate with yourself during each step of the way as you navigate this process.

Conventional Medicine

While medication is one of the most common treatment approaches for ADHD, it's essential to note the fact that around 30% of people with ADHD don't respond to conventional stimulant medication. The second line of treatment consists in non-stimulants; these tend to be even less effective, with around 50% of people not responding to them.[1]

In addition, it's important to understand what to realistically expect from medication when it *does* work. ADHD medication helps to significantly improve symptoms, like attention and focus, for as long it's active in the body, but it doesn't cure ADHD itself—there *is* no cure for it. It's not like fighting an infection and receiving a treatment that eventually gets rid of it. ADHD medication helps regulate neurotransmitter levels, like dopamine or norepinephrine, which, in turn, help improve attention and focus, reduce impulsivity, and enhance executive function.

When considering medication, having an honest and extensive discussion with your doctor is essential. Discuss your treatment expectations and goals, and be open about your symptoms, experiences, and any concerns you may have. Explain how your symptoms impair your daily functioning in order to determine if medication might help. Don't be afraid to ask as many questions as possible about potential medications—their benefits, side effects, and any lifestyle adjustments required—so that you get clear about the best path forward.

Conventional ADHD medicines consist of **stimulants** and **non-stimulants**.

1. **Stimulant medication** like Ritalin (methylphenidate) and Adderall (amphetamine) is the first line of treatment, and it's the most prescribed medication for managing ADHD symptoms.

How stimulants work: Stimulants increase neurotransmitter levels, mainly dopamine and norepinephrine, in the brain. Since dopamine supports motivation and focus, and norepinephrine regulates wakefulness and alertness, these neurotransmitters are key in regulating attention, impulse control, and executive functions.

Effectiveness: They're often highly effective and can provide rapid relief from ADHD symptoms.

Duration: Their effects typically last for just a few hours, so they must be taken multiple times a day in various forms (short acting or long acting) to maintain symptom control. Typically, short-acting forms last around four hours. In comparison, long-acting ones last six to twelve hours, but this can vary depending on each individual and their metabolism.

Unfortunately, over time, the brain may adapt to the flood of neurotransmitters, leading to reduced efficacy and the need for higher doses.

Potential side effects: These include appetite loss, insomnia, headaches, anxiety, mood swings, increased heart rate, and blood pressure.

2. Non-stimulant medication is generally considered when stimulants aren't effective or cause unwanted side effects.

How non-stimulants work: Non-stimulants don't directly increase dopamine. Medication like Strattera (atomoxetine) works by inhibiting the reabsorption of norepinephrine in brain synapses so that there's more available for communication between neurons.

Effectiveness: Non-stimulants are slower acting but are still preferred by some people. However, they can take a few weeks before reaching full efficacy.

Duration: Unlike stimulants, their effects last throughout the day with just a single dose. For this reason, they're more convenient for some people.

Potential side effects: These include fatigue, irritability, drowsiness, and stomach upset.

When you start noticing relief from your symptoms and begin experiencing improved focus and mood, better memory, enhanced attention to detail, reduced impulsivity, and better sleep, it means that the medication is working. If there's little to no improvement in symptoms or you experience any side effects, it's a clear sign that your medication or dosage needs adjustment. Remember, finding the right drug in the right dosage is a process of trial and error, and it can generally take from a few weeks to even six months.

Without a doubt, conventional medication can provide significant help, but it's only one way to address ADHD. Also, it isn't always aligned with everyone's needs and values when it comes to managing their health. That said, let's explore our options a little further.

Complementary Medicine

In this world of instant gratification and quick fixes, it's easy to think that taking care of your health is simply about popping a few pills, but this couldn't be further from the truth. For this reason, we'll now delve into alternative approaches and explore how some medicinal herbs, nutrition, and other holistic practices may have a significant and transformative role in reducing symptoms and improving the lives and well-being of women living with ADHD. Whether you're seeking complementary options in conjunction with conventional treatment or searching for an alternative path altogether, the next few pages will help you explore the avenues that complementary medicine and other holistic practices offer.

13 Natural Remedies for ADHD

In this section, I've included some of the most promising natural remedies. These have been extensively studied and shown to provide many benefits to the nervous system, improve brain function, and reduce ADHD-specific symptoms. Some of these herbs are wonderful for supporting focus and attention, some help stabilize the mood and energize the body, while others are effective for symptoms like insomnia and mental tension.

One thing that I'd like to mention beforehand is that medicinal herbs work slightly different compared to synthetic drugs, in the sense that the active compounds in plants tend to be in much smaller quantities. Therefore, it may take longer sometimes to notice any kind of improvement. I think it's essential to be aware of this aspect, in order to manage expectations when following natural treatments.

1. **Lion's mane** *(Hericium erinaceus)* is a mushroom that's well-known for improving cognitive function, including memory, focus, and alertness. It contains active compounds, such as hericenones and erinacines, that support overall brain health and protect against neurodegeneration. One of its most prominent properties is its capacity to stimulate nerve growth factor (NGF) production. This bioprotein has an essential role in the maintenance and regeneration of neurons in the brain. Lion's mane also has mood-regulating properties, helping decrease emotional fluctuations and improve emotional stability. People who consistently consume lion's mane often report reduced irritability and anxiety.

In my experience of taking Lion's mane, the first effects I noticed were decreased anxiety and an overall sense of calmness. On top of that, I was also able to better maintain my train of thought and recall things much easier.

2. **Ginkgo** *(Ginkgo biloba)* has been shown in various studies[2] to enhance memory, attention, and cognition, as well as promote the repair of damaged brain cells. Also, the powerful antioxidants in ginkgo leaves help protect brain cells from oxidative stress. In addition, ginkgo helps improve blood circulation, allowing more oxygen to reach the brain.

3. Rhodiola *(Rhodiola rosea)* is a medicinal herb that enhances endurance and alertness, helping one to stay focused and energized throughout the day. It's known to lift one's mood and reduce symptoms of depression, as well as increase productivity by enhancing cognitive function. Moreover, this adaptogen herb helps increase the body's resistance to stress, making it more resilient to everyday physical and mental challenges.

4. Ginseng root *(Panax ginseng)* is renowned for its ability to increase energy and combat fatigue. As an adaptogen, ginseng helps the body manage stress better and reduces its negative impacts on the body. The active compounds in ginseng, known as ginsenosides, help enhance dopamine levels and receptor activity, ultimately improving mood, focus, memory, and mental clarity.

5. Brahmi *(Bacopa monnieri)* is a highly appreciated Ayurvedic herb that shows promise for managing ADHD symptoms. It has a long history of use as a cognitive enhancer, helping to improve memory and focus. Beyond its cognitive benefits, bacopa has adaptogenic properties—it helps reduce stress and anxiety, as well as promotes overall mental well-being. It also helps stabilize mood and mitigate symptoms of depression. Moreover, due to being rich in antioxidants, Brahmi has neuroprotective effects that help protect brain cells from oxidative damage.

6. Gotu kola *(Centella asiatica)*. In some Indian folk traditions, it's believed that elephants possess exceptional memory and longevity due to Gotu kola being a staple green in their diet. This herb has a long history of traditional use, and is now supported by modern research. Gotu kola is a nourishing herb for the mind, helping enhance memory and improve blood circulation in the brain. Its antioxidant effects protect the brain from the negative effects of free radicals and aging. Studies[3] show that it promotes neurogenesis (encourages new brain cell growth) and increased cognitive abilities, including learning capacity, attention span, mental endurance, clarity, and focus. It also helps calm the nervous system, ease insomnia, relieve stress and anxiety, and improve mood.

7. **Lemon Balm** *(Melissa officinalis)* has a gentle but effective impact on the mind, which makes it a valuable ally to the ADHD brain. It promotes relaxation and alleviates anxiety, stress, and tension. Its calming effects help ease a racing mind and improve focus.

8. **Eleuthero** *(Eleutherococcus senticosus),* also known as Siberian ginseng, helps elevate mood and reduce feelings of anxiety and irritability. As an adaptogen herb, it enhances resilience to stress and reduces its effects on mental health. Eleuthero is valued for its ability to enhance mental clarity and alertness, improve memory function, increase energy levels, and combat mental fatigue.

9. **Ashwagandha** *(Withania somnifera)* is another wonderful adaptogenic herb known for nourishing the adrenals, thereby reducing the effects of stress and fatigue. It also helps stabilize the mood and alleviate symptoms of depression and anxiety. In addition, this adaptogen has been shown to reduce brain fog, improve sleep quality, and boost overall energy levels and mental vitality.

10. **Valerian root** *(Valeriana officinalis)* promotes a sense of calm and an enhanced mood. It has a calming effect on the nervous system, helping soothe an overactive mind, and it alleviates stress, anxiety, irritability, tension, and nervousness. Due to its mild sedative properties, valerian root helps ease hyperactivity and improves sleep disturbances associated with ADHD.

11. Maca root *(Lepidium meyenii)* is an adaptogenic herb that promotes overall well-being by lowering cortisol levels and improving the body's ability to cope with stress, enhancing mental resilience and vitality. Maca also helps boost mood, mental clarity, memory, and energy.

12. Rosemary *(Rosmarinus officinalis)* is known for improving blood circulation and helping lift low energy and alleviate irritable mood. Rosemary has also been shown to improve memory recall speed.

13. Nettle *(Urtica dioica)* is rich in minerals and vitamins that help enhance and stabilize energy levels. Since it's quite a common herb, many people don't give it too much credit, but be prepared to be surprised in the best way possible. Because it is such a nourishing plant, nettle can be used as a natural supplement whenever there are deficiencies in vitamins and minerals.

For those looking to expand their knowledge on the above mentioned medicinal plants, the full list of studies supporting their benefits and properties is included in the reference section at the end of this book.

Therapy

Therapy plays a vital role alongside medication in managing ADHD. Medication helps address the physiological aspects, whereas therapy equips people with valuable coping strategies and a deeper understanding of the condition.

As the old phrase goes, "Pills don't teach skills!". While medication generally helps improve some ADHD symptoms, like attention and impulsivity, it cannot address skill deficits or help build coping strategies that every person with ADHD will likely require in order to navigate life effectively.

Cognitive behavioral therapy (CBT) is generally the first choice of therapy for ADHD. It focuses on identifying unhelpful thought and behavior patterns, challenging distorted thinking, and adopting more helpful behaviors.

CBT techniques can include examining core beliefs, role-playing situations to practice new behavioral responses, developing organizational systems (planners, calendars, to-do lists) as well as learning to set achievable and measurable goals.

Another type of therapy is dialectical behavior therapy (DBT), which can particularly help with emotional dysregulation. It targets specific things such as impulsivity, irregular moods, and emotional sensitivity.

DBT employs techniques like mindfulness, meditation, and emotional regulation strategies, alongside practicing interpersonal skills. These methods teach therapy patients how to better communicate their needs and set boundaries, improve self-awareness and cope more effectively with mood swings and impulsivity.

Coaching is another common way to address ADHD challenges, particularly those related to executive functioning. Coaching is quite similar to CBT, and it typically focuses on teaching practical strategies that can be implemented to manage symptoms and improve overall daily functioning. You collaborate with your coach to set milestones related to your productivity, time management, and life goals. Coaching is solutions-focused, aiming to provide the missing executive function skills that ADHD clients often lack.

What to Look For in a Therapist?

As with anything else, not all therapists are created equally. Specialization in ADHD among mental health professionals will vary, so always make sure to enquire about their expertise. It's essential to seek out therapists who have significant ADHD training and experience. Once you've found a few solid options, schedule consultations with each to determine the one who will suit you best in terms of personality and approach. You want someone that "gets you." The relationship you have with your therapist matters more than you can imagine—you can have the "best" therapist in the world with the most training and experience, but if they're not the right fit for you, it won't matter in the slightest.

Below are a few examples of questions to ask a potential future therapist, which will assist in determining if they're suitable for you:

- What's your experience with treating ADHD clients? How many years of practice do you have?
- What kind of therapeutic approaches do you use?
- How often would we meet, and for how long each time?
- What are your rates?
- How will therapy help with my ADHD-related struggles?
- How do you involve family in treatment plans?
- Will you be available between sessions if needed? If so, how?

You'll know that you found a suitable therapist if you look forward to your appointments, and if after your therapy sessions you feel more optimistic. The right mental health specialist should make you feel comfortable enough so that you can be completely open and honest about what you're going through.

It can take about three or four sessions before you're able to establish a relationship with a new therapist. By this time, you should be able to gauge if they're the right fit for you or if it's time to go back to your search.

At some point during therapy, however, your therapist can start to feel perhaps a little *too* comfortable. If your sessions no longer challenge you, it may cause your progress to plateau, and that might be a sign that it's time to change to a new one.

Creating a Healthy Lifestyle: Nutrition, Exercise & Sleep

Reducing ADHD symptoms and fully tapping into our potential requires looking at our lifestyle holistically. We've already explored medication, therapy, and alternative natural remedies, and while these are powerful tools, it's crucial to know that there are other things we can implement to alleviate ADHD symptoms, such as lifestyle changes. In the following pages, you'll discover how small tweaks to your nutrition, exercise, and sleep can help to profoundly reduce your symptoms.

PROPER NUTRITION + ADEQUATE SLEEP +
CONSISTENT EXERCISING

=

BETTER ATTENTION AND FOCUS

What Does an ADHD-Friendly Diet Look Like?

First, let's clarify something: There is no food that'll cure ADHD. But without a doubt, there's a strong connection between our diet and the severity of our ADHD symptoms. The right foods will reduce many unwanted symptoms of ADHD due to the nutrients they provide to the body and brain. On the other hand, poor nutrition will exacerbate them.

Let's examine some general nutrition guidelines that can help reduce symptoms and improve our well-being.

1. Consume more protein-rich foods.

Incorporate lean protein[4] into every meal—you'll prevent blood sugar spikes and crashes throughout the day, which can often lead to difficulties sustaining focus. Moreover, a high protein diet helps optimize brain function, as protein provides amino acids like L-tyrosine, a precursor of dopamine and norepinephrine. Some excellent protein sources are beans, eggs, Greek yogurt, cheese, meat, and nuts.

The general rule of thumb is that most adults should consume about 0.75g of protein daily for each kilogram of their body weight, which amounts to approximately two portions of meat, fish, tofu, or nuts each day. As a guideline, a protein portion should fit in the palm of your hand.

2. Increase healthy fats.

Essential fatty acids like omega-3 and omega-6 have been linked to improved concentration and memory.[5] Healthy fats play a crucial role in supporting cognitive function, as they're integral components of brain cell membranes. Also, omega-3s are essential in reducing inflammation in the brain and body, which helps optimize neurotransmitter activity. Some rich sources of healthy fats include fatty fish (salmon, tuna, sardines, mackerel, etc.), walnuts, soybeans, tofu, and avocados.

3. Eat fresh, whole foods.

The more food you have on your plate that comes from nature and not from a factory, the better. Focus on consuming as many fresh, unprocessed foods as possible—they provide the balanced nutrition essential for a healthy brain. Make sure to eat at least four to five servings of veggies and fruits per day, as they help nourish the body with antioxidants, vitamins, and minerals. Avoid foods filled with artificial colorings, flavors, preservatives, refined sugar, and sweeteners that, in various studies[6], have been shown to contribute to ADHD symptoms. These should be limited to the minimum or—even better— removed from the diet completely.

Also, consider nurturing your gut flora with probiotic foods like yogurt, kefir, sauerkraut, kimchi, and kombucha. It's no secret that there's a strong connection between our gut and our brain, so make sure to maintain your gut health to help balance your mood and focus.

In addition, many people with ADHD are often deficient in certain key nutrients, particularly vitamin D, magnesium, zinc, iron, or B vitamins. These nutrients play a crucial role in neuro-transmitter regulation and cognitive processes. Correcting defi-ciencies and getting adequate amounts of these nutrients through diet and supplements helps optimize nervous system functioning and, therefore, curb some ADHD symptoms.

4. Add more complex carbs to your diet.

Unlike simple carbs which spike blood sugar, complex carbs are digested slower, providing a gradual, sustained release of energy and helps to stabilize mood. Also, the fiber in complex carbs helps with focus and attention by stabilizing blood sugar levels.

Some great sources of complex carbs are:

- Whole grains like quinoa, oats, whole grain pasta, and brown rice

- Fruits like apples, bananas, and oranges
- Starchy vegetables like potatoes, sweet potatoes, peas, and corn
- Beans and legumes like lentils and chickpeas

Reduce or eliminate simple carbs, the ones found in processed foods such as sugary snacks, products made from white flour, white rice, and breakfast cereals, as they lack nutritional density. Refined grains have a high glycemic index, meaning they cause blood sugar highs and lows that impact concentration.

5. Stay hydrated.

Our bodies are around 60% water, and our brains around 80%. So it should be no surprise then that hydration is essential for optimal brain function. Ensure that you stay well-hydrated with plenty of water, and limit (or banish!) sugary drinks that lead to blood sugar spikes and crashes that disrupt focus.

6. Implement a consistent meal routine to avoid impulse eating and help stabilize energy.

Even more so than what we eat, *how* we eat is essential for managing ADHD. Many nutritional problems come from poor meal planning and impulsive eating tendencies. Our strong craving for instant gratification often leads us to reach for processed foods that are high in carbs, sugar, and fat and that lack nutritional value.

Planning ahead is key in curbing these impulses and rash decisions. Set aside time every week to grocery shop and plan meals for the following seven days. Set a consistent day, like Sunday, to prep the meals for the week ahead. Having some healthy snacks on hand—like nuts, fresh fruit, or yogurt—also helps. Routine and preparation ensure that healthy options are readily available, and they reduce the urge to make impulsive nutrition choices driven by hunger.

Aim to eat meals and snacks every three to four hours throughout the day so that the glucose reaches the brain at steady levels for optimal energy and mood.

Following an ADHD-friendly diet shouldn't feel restrictive and unenjoyable. The goal isn't to eat boring, bland foods—it's about identifying several nutritious meal options you genuinely like and look forward to eating. Being able to enjoy the food you consume is fundamental for feeling good, as well as for the long-term sustainability of a diet.

If meal planning feels daunting and you'd like to delegate it to someone else, there's always the option of meal-kit delivery services. This way, you reduce the burden of both grocery shopping and meal planning.

In addition, if you have the possibility, you could also delegate this task to a nutritionist. Professional guidance can be a gamechanger in managing ADHD through nutrition. A nutritionist can create custom eating plans tailored to your goals and needs, address nutrient deficiencies and food sensitivities, recommend supplements, track your progress, and make any necessary adjustments to your meal plan. They can also offer a more in-depth education on how nutrition impacts ADHD, as well as provide valuable insights into the role of certain foods, additives, and dietary patterns in exacerbating or mitigating symptoms.

Healthy Sleep Habits

Sleep is another essential aspect when it comes to managing ADHD. Distraction, restlessness, and emotional dysregulation can worsen without proper restorative shut eye at the end of our day.

Unfortunately, as women with ADHD, we often struggle with sleep problems. Our racing minds keep us from falling asleep, and throughout the night, restless sleep has us tossing and turning. Because of this, most mornings feel like an uphill battle against our snooze buttons. Getting a proper night's sleep is challenging for us, ADHD brains, but it's entirely possible with some planning. Below are a few practical tips to optimize your sleep:

Maintain a consistent bedtime and wake-up schedule, even on weekends. Sleeping in at the end of the week is *so* very tempting, but it only worsens sleepiness and grogginess caused by shifting schedules. The reward of a restful, refreshing night of sleep is so worth it! If you do need to make up for some lost sleep, it's better to take a one- or two-hour daytime nap rather than sleeping until later and disrupting your circadian rhythm.

Bedtime should be around the time we naturally feel tired, and once we set a consistent sleep schedule, we should be able to wake up without an alarm. If after a few weeks of keeping a consistent schedule, a morning alarm is still needed, then our bedtime is likely too late and we sleep less than our body needs.

Develop a relaxing pre-bed routine like reading, gentle yoga, or meditation. Limit screen time for one or two hours before bed, as the blue light emitted from our devices impairs melatonin release. Even dim lights can disrupt sleep, so it's best to decrease the use of all electronics that have a digital screen as bedtime approaches. Also, try as much as possible to keep any pre-sleep activities low-key, and avoid stressful work, activities, or conversations before bed.

If you cannot eliminate stimulants like caffeine or sugar completely from your diet, make sure that their consumption doesn't interfere with your sleep by consuming them *at least* four to six hours before bedtime.

Create an ideal sleep environment. Aside from making sure that your bedroom is completely dark, you should also consider setting a cool temperature—the perfect sleep temperature is around 60-68° Fahrenheit (16-20° Celsius). Temperature may seem like an unimportant aspect, but a cool environment is essential for enjoying a deep, restful sleep.

If you struggle with falling asleep, try magnesium supplements before bed, as magnesium helps induce relaxation. Diffusing some relaxing essential oils like lavender in your room can also be useful, as well as drinking a nice cup of warm chamomile, lavender, or lemon balm tea about one to two hours before tucking yourself in.

Exercise

Physical activity may be a general recommendation for health, but for ADHD people, it's more than that—it's an absolute must. Exercise is an essential tool that helps us optimize our brain, mood, and attention. It boosts neurotransmitter levels in the brain—dopamine, norepinephrine, and serotonin—which play essential roles in regulating our focus, memory, and mood. Essentially, physical activity works the same way as Ritalin and Adderall, except that you don't need a prescription for it and it doesn't involve any potential side effects. It's a natural (and free!) method to reduce our ADHD symptoms, and so it would be foolish of us not to take advantage of its benefits. As John Ratey, M.D. and associate clinical professor of psychiatry at Harvard Medical School, said: "Think of exercise as medication. For a small handful of people with ADHD, it may actually be a replacement for stimulants, but for most, it's complementary—something they should absolutely do, along with taking meds, to help increase attention and improve mood."

When it comes to exercising, a key aspect is engaging in something that you genuinely enjoy. For instance, I strongly dislike going to the gym. I find it extremely boring, and being indoors with a bunch of sweaty strangers just isn't my cup of tea. It would be foolish of me to think that I could make a long-term habit out of going to the gym. It's not for me, and that's ok! There are plenty of other options. Over the years, I've found that I enjoy activities like cycling, yoga, and swimming. I like being outdoors and surrounded by nature. While I might not be able to go cycling or swimming consistently, I do make sure I take at least 30 minutes a day to go to the park close to my house for some stretching and light exercise. Because I prefer the overall process of this type of exercise, as well as the feeling afterward, I'm more motivated and likely to engage in it consistently.

Now don't get me wrong—there are some days when I really don't feel like exercising—not one bit. But at the very least, I'll put my training shoes on and decide to go for a walk in the park. I'll also take along some elastic bands and a jumping rope with me, just in case I eventually come around and decide to engage in a workout later on! But at the bare minimum, I've gone outside and got my body moving. Even the smallest bit of physical activity is better than none at all.

And here's the trick: Simply because I've done the hardest part, which is convincing myself to get out of the house and putting my training shoes on, 99% of the time I end up doing a bit of exercise too, whether it's 20 minutes of stretching, light exercise, an elastic bands routine, or jumping rope. I sometimes leave the house feeling so low in energy and dreading just the thought of exercise, but when I'm back from my short workout, I feel re-energized and oh-so happy that I did it.

So figure out what moves you! Find those activities that let you channel your excess energy while also bringing you joy. If you dislike the gym like I do, what do you prefer? Is it running? Dance classes? Cycling out in nature? Just make sure that whatever kind of exercise you decide on, you start out small. Gradual improvements are best in order for these changes to stick long term and feel manageable.

KEY TAKEAWAYS

1. ADHD medicines fall into two categories: stimulants and non-stimulants. Stimulants provide fast-acting symptom relief, but the downside is that their effects wear off quicker and multiple doses are needed throughout the day. Non-stimulants, on the other hand, have a slower onset, but their effects persist throughout the day with just a single dose.

2. Around 30% of people with ADHD don't respond to stimulant medication, and about 50% don't respond to non-stimulants, which highlights the need for additional treatment and therapy options.

3. There are many medicinal plants—ginkgo biloba, lion's mane, ginseng, rhodiola, etc.—that can help optimize the nervous system function and reduce ADHD symptoms. Also, their benefits are supported by science.

4. While medication can help with the physiological aspects of ADHD, therapy is essential for building coping skills, self-awareness, and an overall understanding of the emotional side of the condition.

5. Adjustments in nutrition, sleep, and exercise are crucial for managing and alleviating symptoms. In the context of ADHD, these should be regarded not only as general health recommendations but also as complementary ways to address symptoms.

3

OVERCOMING ADHD-RELATED LIMITING SELF-BELIEFS

"The first problem for all of us is not to learn, but to unlearn."
— Gloria Steinem, American journalist and social activist

*a*s women with ADHD, we commonly battle feelings of self-doubt and inadequacy due to the struggle to meet societal expectations, which leads to a persistent sense of not being good enough. We internalize negative self-beliefs from the stigma and challenges we experience growing up undiagnosed. These negative thoughts become like recordings playing over and over in our minds, undermining our confidence and potential bit by bit.

Living undiagnosed with ADHD leads to years of harsh self-judgment and demoralizing beliefs about ourselves. We internalize that we're fundamentally lazy, stupid, or not enough, not realizing that our challenges are due to a neurodevelopmental disorder and not due to personal shortcomings.

So before diving into the meat of this book, where we'll explore strategies and techniques for managing symptoms and improving executive function, this chapter is a necessary precursor, as it's essential to first address all these destructive narratives fueled by our ADHD challenges.

Changing the Narrative Around ADHD

Do you remember the wave of relief that washed over you when that four-letter diagnosis of "A-D-H-D" finally validated your lifelong struggles? Perhaps you even cried at finally having an explanation for the disconnect you've felt since childhood (I know I did!) or felt lighter knowing that you weren't just "lazy" or "scatterbrained" like you'd been told.

Being diagnosed with ADHD is often hugely cathartic. The validation of having a name for your challenges is *priceless*. It comes with a deep sense of relief: "FINALLY, an explanation for all the difficulties I've faced throughout my life!"

But this was merely the first step into the journey, wasn't it? Now you're embarking on a process of fully accepting ADHD with compassion rather than shame, and unwinding the stigma, misconceptions, and judgments you likely internalized growing up undiagnosed.

Self-acceptance isn't about settling for less, nor is it about resigning. It's about embracing the fullness of who you are and recognizing that *you are enough*. It's about refraining from fighting a part of yourself that'll always be present and allowing you to embrace the positive aspects that ADHD brings. Acceptance means acting from a peaceful place and mindset, acknowledging your worth despite all your differences and challenges. Acceptance means being less critical and negative toward yourself and acting with patience from a place of under-standing.

More importantly, acceptance isn't something that happens overnight just because someone told you to be more open and accepting of your difficulties. It means sitting with your challenges, taking the time to understand them, and, ultimately, working toward improvement. It means less harsh criticism and more "I will try again tomorrow to get better at all the things that I'm struggling with, bit by bit."

Exploring Your Limiting Self-Beliefs

We have all these beliefs that undermine our self-esteem and fill us with shame. The longer they persist unexamined, the more they reinforce self-sabotaging behaviors. By identifying our limiting beliefs and challenging their validity, we can slowly start reshaping our self-talk. We need to start recognizing these narratives for what they are: distorted perceptions of ourselves. They aren't reality.

With self-compassion, self-awareness, and more balanced thinking, we can construct identities based on our strengths and not our struggles. Rewriting old stories frees us and allows us to live life more fully and authentically. By cultivating more empowering perspectives, we slowly start crushing those restrictive, inaccurate views of ourselves.

Overcoming internalized limiting beliefs and stigma isn't an easy process. Still, it's something we need to do in order to fully accept ourselves. It may be a challenging path, but it's most definitely worth the effort. We all deserve to believe in ourselves and all that we can achieve!

Beliefs and How They're Formed

Essentially, our beliefs are the perceptions, assumptions, and opinions we hold to be true about ourselves, others, and the world around us.

Beliefs about ourselves can be positive, such as "I'm a lucky person" or "Most people are nice to me," but they can also be negative, like "I'm always late" or "I can never seem to do anything right."

Our belief system is built based on past experiences and the meanings we've attributed to those events. It's the lens through which we view the world.

We start forming beliefs very early in our childhood when, unfortunately, we don't have much understanding of the world or adequate critical-thinking skills and self-awareness. Therefore, we often reach adulthood harboring some personal views that end up sabotaging us.

For instance, very early in school, we likely received negative feedback on our abilities from our teachers. By taking in that feedback and internalizing it, we might've formed beliefs along the lines of, "I'm stupid" or "I'm not good with numbers." Often, beliefs arise from early experiences such as this, and even if years later we become a completely different person, those beliefs continue to shape our reality.

Recently, I was having a conversation with a fellow ADHD lady. At some point during our chat, she said something like, "I'm not a punctual person. No matter how much I've tried, I just can't be on time." Needless to say, this is quite a strong and negative belief.

As ADHDers, no doubt we have a tendency to underestimate how long some things may take us, which often results in us being late. But the big issue occurs when we internalize and identify with these beliefs so deeply that we don't give ourselves any chance of ever getting past them.

One of the strongest forces in human psychology is the need to remain congruent with how we see ourselves. In the same way that computers operate based on software, we only operate based on the programs (beliefs) that we have. Our behaviors will never change beyond the limitations of our programming.

"I am" statements can be really empowering when used correctly but incredibly dangerous when referring to limiting behaviors. When we say the same negative thing to ourselves over and over, we only reinforce it and continue to erode our self-esteem and self-worth. As a result, we start feeling more and more anxiety, depression, and hopelessness. We need to avoid becoming too attached to a certain belief that doesn't serve us. But how do we do this?

Well, it's best to think of beliefs as working hypotheses— merely theories that can either be proven or disproven. For example, a much healthier way to refer to some of our short-comings without making them part of our identity (and ulti-mately having them become self-fulfilling prophecies) is to transform an affirmation like "I'm not punctual" into "I some-times struggle with punctuality, but I'm working on improv-ing." How much more room does that give us to work with? A lot! This way, we don't negate that we have an issue with punc-tuality and go overboard with affirmations like "I'm a punctual person," despite never making it to an appointment on time in our entire lives. But we also don't get too attached to this type of behavior or theory that we have over ourselves. Remember: Reality is never what it is, but rather our perspective on what we *think* it is.

Examining our beliefs and understanding where they originate from is so important in order to build self-awareness, and transforming limiting beliefs is crucial for changing unwanted behaviors and thought patterns.

For this to happen, it's essential that we understand the cycle of beliefs. It goes like this: our beliefs dictate our thoughts, our thoughts influence our feelings, our feelings influence our actions, and, ultimately, bring in results that only reinforce our existing beliefs. And the cycle continues over and over. Because of this, most people find themselves stuck in a never-ending cycle of similar events and results. No matter what they try to change on the surface, the deeply rooted beliefs will always prevail.

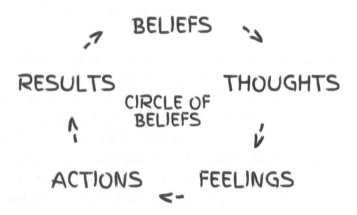

The easiest way to spot your beliefs about yourself and the world is by looking at your life and observing the areas in which you struggle the most.

The Most Common Negative Beliefs of Women With ADHD

We internalize so many limiting beliefs that stem from our symptoms. We've exemplified a few so far, but let's go over a more extensive list of some of the most frequent ones:

- "I'm lazy."
- "I'm disorganized."
- "I'm a procrastinator."
- "I'm not a punctual person."
- "I'm not intelligent."
- "I'm hypersensitive."
- "I'm overly emotional."
- "I'm inherently flawed or broken."
- "I'm not trying hard enough."
- "I'm not good enough."
- "I'm unworthy of love/acceptance/joy, etc."
- "I'm socially awkward."
- "There's something fundamentally wrong with me."
- "I'm a failure."
- "I'll never achieve my goals and dreams."

The destructive beliefs that ADHD challenges can trigger deeply undermine our confidence in our abilities to fulfill our full potential—and no wonder! When we see ourselves as inherently incompetent, lazy, unintelligent, and never good enough, it impacts every area of our lives. It affects our motivation, making us think that we shouldn't even bother trying since we'll just mess up anyway. Negative self-talk also impacts our mental health and fills us with shame, which further triggers feelings of anxiety and depression. It influences our behavior, making us not want to put effort into improving because we see our situation and whole persona through the lens of hopelessness. We feel broken and we stop seeking growth, which limits our potential. It also negatively impacts our relationships—the simple beliefs that we're unlikeable, awkward, or annoying become self-fulfilling prophecies. This, ultimately, makes us want to avoid rejection and isolate ourselves.

Ultimately, our core beliefs shape our self-esteem and behavior. They dictate how we move through the world and what we allow ourselves to accomplish, and this is why re-examining our beliefs and assumptions is critical.

Now, considering the cycle of beliefs above, let's use the common belief "I'm lazy" as an example:

- **Belief:** "I'm lazy."
- **Thoughts:** "Why bother trying? I'll never get anything done anyway" or "I'm too lazy to start working on this."
- **Feelings:** Apathy, hopelessness, and demotivation
- **Actions:** Because you feel demotivated and hopeless, you end up procrastinating, avoiding tasks, and not initiating any work. You instead become distracted with easy activities like scrolling through social media or watching TV.
- **Results:** The consequences of your actions are failing to meet deadlines or accomplishing less than you'd like. Ultimately, the result you get reaffirms the initial belief that you're lazy.

How do we change these limiting beliefs and get unstuck from our patterns? Here's how to break these negative cycles:

1. **Become aware of your limiting beliefs.** If you're not entirely sure how to identify them, simply think of limiting beliefs as limiting repetitive thoughts. During your day, become aware of

any of these thought patterns and cognitive distortions, and then take note of them.

2. Examine a belief's origins. Explore when and where a particular belief may have started. Is there any evidence supporting it?

3. Challenge your beliefs. Start by recognizing that a certain belief may not be entirely accurate or fair. Instead of labeling yourself as lazy, acknowledge that while you may struggle with motivation at times, it doesn't define your identity. Develop more balanced thoughts. Also, take a few moments to write out a piece of evidence to the contrary. For example, "My boss has said on a few occasions how much he appreciates me for my hard-working nature. Therefore, it's not realistic for me to say a general statement like "I'm lazy."

4. Replace negative self-talk with more uplifting statements. Focus less on your struggles and reframe them to a better version that sounds realistic, such as "Sometimes, I may not be very productive, but I'm taking small steps to improve."

5. Set small goals. By achieving these mini goals, you build confidence and gradually create a positive cycle. When you experience small achievements over and over, you provide evidence that supports a more constructive belief.

6. Track your progress. Keep a journal to record your accomplishments, no matter how small they may be. The tangible evidence will challenge the initial belief and show that you are, in fact, capable of productivity.

7. Seek support. Sometimes, we may live with the impression that we have to deal with our struggles all by ourselves, but this shouldn't be the case. Most often, family and friends are happy to offer support, so allow them to help out. Talk to your loved ones or a therapist about your struggles. They can provide accountability and encouragement, offer insights, and make it easier for you to stay on the right track. Plus, surrounding yourself with people who love you and see your full potential helps reinforce your qualities and strengths. Their more positive perspective on you can have a significant role in shaping your self-image.

By following this process, you can gradually shift your belief system, leading to more positive thoughts, emotions, actions, and results. By putting in consistent awareness and effort, you'll slowly dismantle those negative old stories you've been telling yourself for so long and that have been holding you back. Every small shift in perspective helps build momentum, ultimately helping you break free from the restrictive roles you've boxed yourself into.

With consistency and patience, you'll be able to overcome these damaging self-beliefs. It takes time to rewrite old mental scripts, so show yourself grace throughout the process. When we chip away at these limiting narratives and build more empowering ones, we unlock a new level of well-being, self-confidence in our abilities, resilience, better relationships, improved mental health, and, ultimately, better life satisfaction.

This process requires a lot of perseverance, courage, and a solid dose of self-compassion. It's vital to keep in mind that your progress won't be linear, and that each small shift toward a more balanced perspective will build momentum. The journey toward living fully and freely begins from within.

KEY TAKEAWAYS

1. Destructive narratives stem from early struggles and repeated failures, and with time, they become tightly woven into our self-image.

2. Our belief system is like the software we run on or the lens through which we view the world. We always act in congruency with our beliefs.

3. We must cultivate self-awareness around our beliefs, and challenge the ones that don't serve us and keep us limited.

4. Replacing limiting narratives with positive ones will gradually help us improve our thoughts, emotions, actions, and, ultimately, our results in life. This change builds more self-confidence, better mental health, relationships, and a more fulfilling life overall.

5. Receiving an ADHD diagnosis can bring immense relief and a sense of validation, marking the first step into your ADHD journey. What follows is internal work on accepting it. Acceptance is by no means settling for less, but instead fully embracing who you are, with all the good and—perhaps more importantly—the bad. It means taking the time to understand your challenges and to work toward improvement each day.

4

HOW TO NAVIGATE EXECUTIVE FUNCTION CHALLENGES

"If you can't fly, then run; if you can't run, then walk; if you can't walk, then crawl, but whatever you do, you have to keep moving forward."
— Martin Luther King Jr., American minister and activist

*L*ife as a woman with ADHD is a whirlwind of unpredictability. From forgetfulness to hyperfocus and from missed appointments to the thrill of a new project, every day feels like a rollercoaster ride—and sometimes not the fun kind. This daily rollercoaster often feels more dizzying than thrilling. But remember, you're not alone in this journey, and many other women with ADHD struggle with the same things you do. Your struggles don't define you, and there isn't anything inherently wrong with you as a person (I'll remind you and repeat this as many times as is necessary!).

More importantly, there are many CBT techniques and coping strategies you can use to improve your symptoms, which we'll explore in this chapter.

Executive Functions

Understanding what executive functions are and the challenges caused by ADHD is an essential step when seeking to lessen the severity of your symptoms.

Simply put, executive functions are the mental processes that manage planning, organizing, initiating tasks, shifting attention, regulating emotions, inhibiting impulses, and working memory. These functions allow us to pursue goals, make decisions, solve problems, and adapt to new situations. They play a crucial role in productivity, academic performance, relationships, and our overall functioning and quality of life. Executive functions start developing in infancy and continue to do so until we reach early adulthood.

ADHD is believed to cause executive dysfunction by affecting the brain's reward circuit, which leads to well-known challenges in regulating attention, emotions, and behavior. It's estimated that an astonishing 90% of people diagnosed with ADHD have executive function challenges. (Potts, 2023)

The core executive functions[1] are inhibition, working memory, and cognitive flexibility.

1. **Inhibition** refers to the ability to control impulses, thoughts, and behaviors. A person with ADHD often finds it difficult to inhibit inappropriate actions or responses, which leads to impulsive behaviors, heightened emotional reactions, and poor self-control.

2. **Working memory** refers to the capacity to temporarily retain and mentally process information in order to complete tasks.

ADHD, unfortunately, brings challenges related to working memory, and therefore, our ability to remember information, stay focused on tasks, or follow multi-step instructions is affected.

3. Cognitive flexibility refers to the ability to adapt to new situations and environments and switch focus between tasks or stimuli. Most of us with ADHD encounter challenges in this aspect. We commonly have difficulties transitioning between activities and adapting to changes, are easily distracted, and struggle with multitasking, problem solving, and shifting attention.

These core executive functions support a range of higher-level functions, including planning, reasoning, problem solving, organizing, task initiation, decision making, time management, focusing, shifting attention, and goal-directed behavior. These are referred to as "higher-level functions" as they require a combination of the core executive functions.

If you're someone who hasn't yet been diagnosed, it's extremely important to note that experiencing executive dysfunction doesn't necessarily mean that you have ADHD. While the two significantly overlap, they're not equivalent. Many other things—like learning disabilities, autism, depression, degenerative conditions, sleep deprivation, brain injuries, and various other environmental, psychological, and genetic factors—could be the root cause of executive dysfunction.

Executive functions can be impacted to varying degrees among people with ADHD. Generally, addressing the deficits related to executive functions requires a combination of therapy, medication, and behavioral strategies, as well as support from family and friends. We've covered therapy and medication options in the previous chapters, so in this one, we'll examine a set of CBT techniques and behavioral strategies that'll help you in your ADHD journey.

Improving Executive Function

The CBT techniques and behavioral strategies I've included here are the ones that I've found to be effective in managing my own ADHD. You may already be familiar with some approaches, or perhaps initially find them to be overly simple. However, I encourage you to try implementing them with an open mind and not to dismiss any of them too soon, as some of the best techniques are the ones that are simple and easy to implement. Also, please don't feel compelled to adopt too many changes at once—trying to overhaul everything simultaneously often brings poor results. Give yourself the time and space to test them one by one, and see which ones work best for you. Consider this guide a toolbox from which you can pick and choose the most useful tools for your needs, and remember that the tips that end up working best will be unique to each person.

Overcoming Your Procrastination Tendencies

Procrastination and lack of motivation are challenging enough for most people, but for us with ADHD brains, these issues are significantly more intense and persistent.

To address these challenges effectively, it's essential first to understand the difference between procrastination and laziness, as they're often mistakenly considered synonymous. Procrastination arises from a feeling of being overwhelmed. It occurs when you intend to complete a task eventually, but you keep postponing it because it feels daunting. In contrast, laziness involves an unwillingness to put in the necessary effort.

People with ADHD are often unfairly labeled as lazy. However, a closer look inside an ADHD mind reveals a sense of overwhelm rather than laziness or a lack of willingness.

Why Do We Procrastinate?

Our brains are wired to keep us in our comfort zone, in familiar territory. This tendency goes back to our ancestors, who had to conserve energy and avoid unnecessary risks in order to survive. While this mechanism was crucial for survival in the past, this evolutionary trait in modern times holds us back from pursuing our goals, wanting to accomplish tasks, and taking on new challenges. This wiring is the reason why we'll choose Netflix over going to the gym or starting on a new project. Our brain perceives these activities that require effort as potentially dangerous, as they take us away from our comfort zone. We intellectually know that there's nothing to fear about starting a new task or exercising. We know that change can often be good, but our primal instincts beg to differ. They want us to be safely nestled, even if that means missing out on opportunities.

Understating this aspect of our brain can help us see that our procrastination tendencies and resistance toward certain tasks aren't a reflection of our abilities but rather a deeply ingrained survival mechanism. Armed with this knowledge, we can start to chip away at the barriers our brains have created.

It's important to acknowledge that the first step in pretty much everything will be met with resistance, but this resistance is not an immutable force. With some persistence, it can be dispersed. But what's the best way to go about this?

To combat procrastination effectively, we need to look into how motivation works. You see, motivation is a fickle thing. We've all experienced that initial spark, a surge of excitement to conquer new challenges, whether related to work goals, hitting the gym, or building better eating habits. However, that drive diminishes as quickly as it arises.

The most common misconception around motivation is that we have to wait for it to strike before we make a move. In reality though, this works the other way around—we have to start with some form of action first, and then motivation will follow behind like a faithful shadow. Want to go out for a jog but don't really feel like it? Start by putting your training shoes on. Do you have work to do but feel overwhelmed by merely thinking about it? Just take a tiny step, like opening your laptop.

ACTION -> MOTIVATION -> MORE MOTIVATION

You've probably noticed that on those slow mornings when you feel like lounging and sleeping in, the entire day tends to adopt a leisurely pace. It's like setting the dial to "chill mode," and then the universe seems to conspire to match that energy. On the flipside, the days when we jump out of bed and into the shower, followed perhaps by an invigorating jog or gym session and then conquering our to-do list, are the ones that sparkle with productivity. Why? Because we've built momentum first thing in the morning. That initial burst of energy sets the tone for the entire day, making our daily tasks feel less daunting. With each completed task, the motivation snowball grows bigger and becomes a force that propels us through our day.

I know very well the temptation of hitting the snooze button when your bed has you wrapped in its warmth and comfort.

However, when you resist that urge, you signal to your brain that it's time for action.

You don't have to deal with anything major first thing in the morning. Begin with something small, a task that's extremely manageable and achievable, like making your bed or watering your plants. While these tasks might seem trivial, they serve as warm-up exercises for your motivation muscles, setting the stage for bigger acts of accomplishment. Remember, momentum isn't about the magnitude of tasks but rather the speed at which you're moving forward. The sense of accomplishment from completing a small task helps build momentum and motivation for the more significant tasks. So as you sip your morning coffee or tea, remember that your choice to start your day sets the rhythm. One step naturally leads to another, and before you know it, you're riding that wave of accomplishment.

How to Stop Getting Overwhelmed by Tasks

Similar to how we build up motivation, we should look at tackling more complex tasks or projects that may feel daunting—by starting with a small, first step.

Task breakdown is a great cognitive strategy. In fact, breaking down tasks is essential in order not to feel overwhelmed by the amount of effort and work that an activity entails. It helps increase clarity and facilitates a systemic approach to completing goals. In addition, completing each subtask will provide a sense of accomplishment, boosting the motivation and momentum to move on to the next step.

The Body Double Technique

To further increase your motivation and productivity (and to get that extra push), use the body double technique. Basically, this method consists of putting yourself in a room where there's somebody else doing what you're supposed to be doing. If you need to exercise, you go to a gym where the collective energy of those around you will help you stay on task when you're tempted to drift away. If you need to clean your house, have your partner or another family member clean with you. If you need to work and focus, find a co-working space or a cozy corner in a library where others also study or work. For instance, throughout the writing process of this book, I frequently found myself seeking alternative places, like co-working spaces or the local library instead of just trying to work from home because distractions or lack of motivation often hindered my productivity. Pushing myself to go into an environment where I'd be surrounded by others working would help me ease into a more productive mood.

How to Improve Time Management

Oftentimes for a woman with ADHD, time can feel like quite an abstract thing. Keeping track of time, meeting deadlines, and managing schedules often feel like an uphill battle. We manage our days through a back-and-forth of sluggish inaction and last-minute frenzy, constantly struggling to find a middle ground conducive to steady progress. However, implementing a few key time-management strategies can provide much-needed structure. Tools like calendars, to-do lists, timers, and alarms help quantify time into well-defined blocks, keep tasks from falling through the cracks, and assist with limiting distractions.

The Power of Accurately Estimating Time

Because of our ADHD brains, we tend to be overly optimistic when it comes to estimating how long things take us. "I'll meet you in 15 minutes," we say, even though we're not even dressed yet and the commute is at least 20 minutes. Sound familiar? I've done this for half of my life!

But I was getting tired of constantly being plagued by the stress of knowing that I wasn't going to make it on time. I was running out of excuses—not to mention that I knew how disrespectful it was toward others to keep them waiting. I knew that I needed to change. So, I started adjusting my schedule to ensure that I'd always arrive 15-30 minutes early at my destinations. This began with timing how long I took to get ready and adding some buffer time to that. I'd use Google Maps to track commute duration, allowing also some extra time in case of traffic. Once I got into this habit, my time-management skills and punctuality improved immeasurably.

At first, I had doubts that I'd ever be able to become a punctual person, considering that from childhood into early adulthood, I was the total opposite of one. But I was wrong. And if I was able to change, you absolutely can too!

Essentially, poor time management comes from a habit of underestimating how long it takes to do something. To address this, time your daily activities for about a week, using your phone's timer app. Ensure to allocate extra time for unforeseen events, be it for commuting, work deadlines, or any other important activities, where delays would have a significant negative impact. It's essential when tracking activity durations, to avoid rushing or speeding up beyond your usual pace. Maintaining your typical speed allows for an accurate assessment of how long each task really takes.

Calendars and To-Do lists

You're likely familiar with the use of calendars and to-do lists. Still, I've included them in this chapter, as there's a chance that you haven't been using them to their full potential. These tools are common for a reason—they're simple and effective. I don't know of anyone who manages their day well and doesn't use at least one of them.

- **To-Do Lists**

You know those moments when you suddenly remember something you need to do, but then a few seconds later your brain pretends that it never happened? Of course you do— we've all been there, my fellow ADHD brains. This is where the oh-so-necessary to-do lists make a world of difference. They serve as daily roadmaps which help us to follow and conquer tasks. So let's look at some essential tips for optimizing your use of this time-management tool:

1. Create your to-do list the night before to save time and maintain your momentum in the morning.

2. Break your daily tasks into manageable chunks. Be realistic with how much you can do in your allocated time, and avoid overloading your list. In the same way that your oven couldn't possibly cook a seven-layer cake in 15 minutes, you also shouldn't pile tasks on your list like you're the mother of multitasking. For instance, if your goal is to create a complete work presentation today, break it down into smaller chunks. Start with "research for presentation" on your initial to-do list, and only after completing that, add the next task to your list.

3. Arrange your to-do items based on urgency and importance (create a prioritized list). Pick your MIT (Most Important

Thing)—the task that moves the needle more than any other for the day. Focus on that, and only move to the next thing once you've tackled your MIT.

4. Assign specific timeframes to each task, so you have a clear endpoint for every to-do item and a designated wrap-up time for your day. Otherwise, you'll notice that tasks expand and spill over into one another, and you'll fall into the trap of "I never have time for myself!" After all, it's your time and mental health at stake here.

Now let's see how this looks in practice. I'll give you as an example one of my recent to-do lists:

To-Do List

- Respond to e-mails
- Water plants
- Conduct research for the next chapter
- Buy groceries
- Go to the post office

Prioritized List

1. Conduct research for the next chapter (MIT): 9 a.m.-1 p.m.
2. Respond to e-mails 2 p.m.-3 p.m.
3. Go to the post office 3 p.m.-3:30 p.m.
4. Buy groceries 3:45 p.m.-5 p.m.
5. Water plants 5:30 p.m.-6 p.m.

As shown in the prioritized list, the MIT for the day involves conducting my research for the next chapter; this is the needle-moving task for that day that ensures my progress. In the case that something comes up and I don't have the time for everything, other less-urgent tasks can be rescheduled, but my MIT is non-negotiable.

So consider to-do lists as your BFFs from this point forward. And, just so you can really see the extent to which I care about you applying this method and benefiting from it, I summarized its steps into a little poem:

Break it down then write it down,

Prioritize and time it—no longer will you frown,

Give your day a curtain call,

And with these steps, you'll accomplish it ALL.

Implement this hack and you'll be a productivity superhero. Pinky promise!

- **Calendars**

If you're serious about time management, using a calendar is essential. You can opt to use the one on your phone, a physical agenda, or Google Calendar—whichever you like best. I prefer using the calendar on my phone because I always have it with me, plus it also syncs with the one on my Mac.

Now, you might think, "Well, if I have a well-structured to-do list, do I really need calendar?" To be honest, it's a matter of choice. You can use either one, and there's absolutely no need for both. In my case, I prefer using a calendar on my busiest days (usually during the workweek), as it helps me keep better track of things. Since you can't set up notifications in your to-do lists the same way you can in your calendar, I find calendars more practical.

To-do lists come in handy during those days when I'm not as pressed for time, like during weekends. They help me remember the tasks I have to complete, but the timeline is more relaxed and I don't require alerts for meetings and reminders. With this in mind, pick the tool that makes the most sense for you—and the one that's most efficient at helping you get stuff done!

How to Minimize Distractions and Improve Focus

Most of the time, attention may not be our superpower as ADHD women (the exception being, of course, our hyperfocus moments). Nonetheless, the ability to focus is a skill that can be refined to a certain extent. On top of the strategies, tools, and techniques examined so far, below are some extra strategies that can help strengthen your focus game:

1. **Avoid multitasking.** Juggling this, that, and the other thing might seem like a way to get more done, but it's akin to having too many balls in the air. Sure, you'll catch a few, but most will end up on the floor. Focus on one thing at a time and give it your undivided attention. In the long term, your productivity will thank you.

2. **Put some boundaries between you and your phone.** Your mobile device is the number one distractor, so silence it, turn off notifications, and, if possible, give it a well-deserved rest in another room. Personally, when I'm not able to keep it in another room, I'll try to at least place it out of my visual radius so that I'm not tempted to check messages or social media.

3. **Optimize your workspace.** If your work involves using a laptop, close any unnecessary tabs and commit to one task. Wearing headphones is also very useful to avoid noise distractions and prevent interruptions. While this might not be feasible for everyone, if it's an option for you, consider listening to deep-focus music or white noise to boost your productivity.

4. Set a timer. Choose a time interval—whether 60 or 90 minutes, whatever floats your focus boat—and give yourself two options: either tackle the task at hand or do nothing. Trust me, you'll find work more exciting than staring at the ceiling. Equally as important, when your set time is up, take a 10-minute break and reward yourself—have a snack, enjoy some tea, or take a short walk.

5. Designate a workspace. For those working from home, it's extremely beneficial to designate another room, other than your bedroom, as your workspace. Keep this area minimal in terms of items and furniture to lessen distractions. Consider it a Zen garden for your brain and productivity. With time, your brain will know that when you enter that space, you need to switch to work mode.

Distractibility Delay

It's interesting how distractions have a way of sneaking in when we're working on difficult or boring tasks. Ever notice that sometimes while tackling an important assignment for work, your thoughts wander to washing the dishes, watering your plants, or booking your weekend getaway flights? These distractions hijack your attention, cleverly convincing you of their urgency, prompting you to handle them before they slip from your mind.

We, as ADHD brains, often struggle to ignore new thoughts that pop up while we're knee-deep in a task. We worry that these new thoughts will quickly disappear, so we immediately act on them at the expense of our focus and productivity. But not anymore. Cue the distractibility delay technique!

What does this method entail? It's simple:

- Let's say that you've allocated a 60-minute block for an important task. During this time, keep a notebook or note-taking app nearby.
- When a distracting thought disrupts your focus, write it down. Don't act on it—just make a note to ensure that you don't forget it.
- After putting it in your notes, swiftly return to your task and stay committed to it until the 60 minutes are over.
- When your allotted task time is up, you can take a break and review the list of notes and decide which ones require your attention and which don't. Did booking your flights really deserve immediate attention or did it just tempt you because it wasn't work related?
- At the end of your workday, you can go over the entire list of distractions, and if any of these items truly deserve your time and attention, you can either act on them or add them to your to-do list for the next day.

This strategy will help you rein in those distractions and regain control of your focus. Your mind might be a playground, but remember: You're the playground supervisor!

How to Improve Your Working Memory

Our mental workspace or working memory is the place where we temporarily store the necessary information for various tasks, like doing mental calculations, following verbal instructions, or remembering a new person's name during a conversation. Enhancing working memory has the potential to improve various aspects of our lives, including decision making, productivity, and social skills.

For ADHD minds, working memory often presents challenges. Because of this, many situations that require us to use our short-term memory can feel like trying to hold sand in our hands. An example of a situation that probably most of us lived through, is the work scenario where the manager outlines a series of action items for a new project. While everyone else seems to grasp the tasks easily, you find yourself struggling to recall all the steps — not because you weren't paying attention or because you're not smart enough, but simply because of ADHD. Our brains are wired differently, functioning in unique ways. Fortunately, working memory is like a muscle that can be strengthened through training. Consistent practice through memory exercises can effectively enhance the mental workspace over time.

Practical Exercises to Improve Working Memory

These types of exercises require you to manipulate familiar information in an unconventional way, boosting your cognitive flexibility and memory abilities.

One of the most common types of exercises requires saying a familiar sequence of words, letters, or numbers *backward*. You can practice these types of exercises any time, for example, while commuting or waiting in line at the grocery store. They may seem a bit mind bending, but that's the point. Get those stagnant brain juices flowing and work that mental muscle! You can perform these aloud or in your mind, but it's effective either way.

Reverse Order Sequences

- Begin with December and say the months of the year backward.

- Start with Monday and recite the days of the week in reverse.
- Start with 60 and count backward by 3's.
- Say the entire alphabet in reverse.
- Start with 100 and count backward by 2's.

Reverse Spelling

Choose a word and spell it backward. For example, try spelling out these in reverse:

- The opposite of small
- The opposite of dark
- A piece of fruit
- A color

The essential aspect of these types of exercises is to ensure that they're challenging enough. If they're too easy, they won't help improve your working memory, and if they're too difficult, they'll just make you feel stressed and frustrated.

The above exercises are just a few examples, but feel free to come up with new words and adjust their difficulty according to your preferences.

Memory Card Game

1. Prepare a deck of playing cards.
2. Shuffle the cards and lay them face down in a grid.
3. Flip two cards over at a time, trying to match pairs.
4. If you find a matching pair, remove them from the grid. If not, flip them back face down.
5. Repeat the process until all pairs are matched.

The card game will engage your working memory by requiring you to remember the location of various cards as you flip them over. The challenge of matching pairs while keeping track of card placements exercises your ability to hold and manipulate information in your short-term memory.

Word List Recall

1. Write down a list of unrelated words (e.g., mug, apple, train, napkin, woman, glasses, tree)
2. Study the list for a brief period, no more than 20 to 30 seconds.
3. Cover the list, and try to recall and write down as many words as you can.
4. Gradually increase the complexity by using more words in a list.

Word list recall exercises enhance your short-term memory by training your brain to retain and recall a sequence of unrelated items. Repeated practice improves your ability to hold onto and reproduce information temporarily.

Story Retelling

1. Read a short story or article.
2. Summarize and retell the story in your own words, covering key points.

Story-retelling exercises engage your working memory by requiring you to recall and convey the main elements of a narrative. This type of practice strengthens your ability to retain and organize information in a coherent manner.

Other well-known games, such as chess, crosswords, jigsaw puzzles, or sudoku, are also helpful in training and improving working memory, focus, and decision making. You can find any of these online for free.

Incorporate a variety of these exercises into your routine in order to improve your working memory. Consistent practice of just a few minutes each day and gradual progression will lead to noticeable improvements in your memory abilities.

Practical Exercises to Optimize Learning and Recall Information Easier

1. Chunking Information

A technique that can assist in easier information recall is breaking it down into small, manageable chunks. For example, when trying to remember a long number, group it into sets of three or four digits, similar to phone numbers (123-456-789), to make it more manageable.

2. Association and Visualization

To practice this method, you'll need to link new information to something you already know or vivid images in order to make it more memorable. For example, let's say that you just met someone named Lily. To remember her name easily, you could visualize her holding a lily flower.

3. The Memory Palace Technique

This method, also often referred to as the "method of loci"[2], is a mental technique that involves imagining an area that you know very well in order to memorize lists of information.

Steps:

- Choose a location that you're very familiar with, such as your house, your office, a local shop, or the park next to your home.
- Map out a specific route through this location. Generally, most people find it helpful to follow a clockwise direction, but this isn't a mandatory aspect.
- Have your list of items that you want to remember.
- Take one or two items at a time and associate them with images, then set these images in a different place along your chosen route.
- Make the images come alive using sensory details, humor and exaggeration, to enhance memorability.

I'll give you an example. Let's say that you need to remember the following list of grocery items: tomatoes, milk, eggs, shampoo, laundry detergent, scissors, and a notebook.

- **Memory palace:** your home
- **Chosen route:** front door > hallway > kitchen > bathroom > bedroom > balcony > balcony chair
- **Items to remember:** tomatoes, milk, eggs, shampoo, laundry detergent, scissors, notebook

The story you could visualize could be something like the following:

You see the front door opening, and all of a sudden, a cascade of giant, ripe tomatoes tumbles out. As you go inside, you see a flowing river of milk running down the hallway that gets onto your feet and makes your socks wet. You go to the kitchen and notice some adorable, fluffy little chicks that laugh while they're launching eggs into the ceiling with slingshots. You then go to the bathroom, and as you enter, you see some mermaids washing their long, wavy hair in your bathtub, which is filled with shampoo bubbles. From there, you go into your bedroom, and you notice two washing machines with human faces, grabbing some green detergent pods and eating them with joy. Suddenly, a little kid comes and takes you to your balcony, where a giant pair of animated scissors playfully trims your plants. You go back into your bedroom, and on your bed, you notice a white owl sitting on top of a giant, open notebook.

Concocting a tale like this sounds a bit out there? A bit "woo-woo?" Well, perhaps for someone who has no trouble remembering things, but for the ADHD brain, a technique like this can be a godsend. By connecting each item to a vivid, imaginative scene in a place that you know well, this memorable storyline makes your grocery list much more engaging and easier to remember. The more creative, absurd, and unique the associations you make, the better they'll stick in your memory and help you recall information.

1. Feynman Technique

The Feynman technique is a study method in which you learn by teaching. You choose a topic you want to understand, then pretend you're teaching someone who knows nothing about this subject. Simplify the material using analogies and examples. This approach helps you identify gaps in your knowledge and breaks down complex ideas. When you struggle to explain something clearly, it indicates areas that you need to review and understand better. You'll then revisit your notes and fill in the gaps in your understanding, and repeat the process until you feel that you can teach the topic easily.

2. Songs and Rhymes

Using rhythm, melody, and repetition can effectively help you recall information. Do you remember the little poem I wrote for you a few pages ago? I used this method to help you remember the steps for creating effective to-do lists more easily.

How to Manage Impulsive Behaviors and Improve Self-Control

Ever found yourself experiencing a rush of excitement about an online sale, and then—BAM!—before you know it, you've bought two new dresses that you didn't actually need? Or perhaps you've been in a work meeting, and suddenly an idea pops into your head and you just blurt it out despite the fact that someone else was speaking? If so, blame it on the inhibitory control. This function acts as a little voice in your head that whispers, "Hold on a second...is this a good idea?" or "Do we really need this?" It's essentially our inner pause button. However, for many of us ADHD women, it can feel as if this pause button on our brain's remote control is missing. As a result, we tend to interrupt conversations, blurt out whatever's on our minds, or impulsively swipe our credit cards, buying stuff we're really excited about but don't actually need.

The Science Behind Impulsive Behavior

The prefrontal cortex is the region of the brain responsible for decision making and self-control, with neurotransmitters such as dopamine and norepinephrine playing a crucial role. Due to imbalances in neurotransmitter levels and communication between brain areas in people with ADHD, the inhibitory function is affected. This contributes to challenges in pausing before taking action, resisting impulses, or maintaining self-control. While our natural inhibitory "muscles" may not be as strong as those of neurotypical people, we can use a few cognitive strategies to reign in our impulses:

The Stop Signal Technique

1. The first step is to identify a common impulsive behavior that you want to work on (emotional spending, for example).
2. Once you've identified the behavior, set up a "stop" cue, such as silently counting to three or taking a deep breath when you feel the urge to buy something that you don't actually need.
3. When you feel the impulse rising, you activate the stop cue by counting or taking a deep breath. This short pause will allow your brain to reconsider the impulsive action.

The Response Cost Technique

1. Choose an impulsive behavior that you want to work on (interrupting others, for example).
2. Decide on a tangible cost or a consequence for engaging in this impulsive behavior, such as putting five dollars in a "penalty jar" every time you interrupt.
3. When you catch yourself engaging in impulsive behavior, you immediately apply the consequence.
4. Over time, the discomfort of the consequence becomes associated with the impulsive action, thereby discouraging it. As the behavior diminishes, you can gradually adjust or remove the consequence.

The penalty amount should be a significant one so that it feels at least a bit painful. Keep in mind that you're not allowed to use that money on yourself, otherwise you'd be rewarding your impulsiveness! Put it towards a nasty bill or donate it to charity instead.

Practice Mindfulness Meditation

1. Set aside a few minutes each day for mindfulness meditation.
2. Find a quiet and comfortable place to sit or lie down.
3. Focus your attention on your breath, acknowledging any impulses or thoughts that arise.
4. Instead of acting on the impulses, observe them non-judgmentally and let them pass.

With consistent practice, mindfulness helps you become more aware of your impulses, providing space to decide whether to act on them or not.

Cognitive Training Games

There are numerous apps out there that are specifically designed to enhance cognitive abilities, such as attention, memory, flexibility, speed of processing, problem-solving, impulse control, etc. Here are a few of these worth exploring:

- Lumosity
- Cogmed
- Peak
- Elevate
- Cognifit
- Brainwell

By engaging in regular practice with the games from these apps you'll be able to improve your cognitive control and reduce impulsivity.

KEY TAKEAWAYS

1. Executive functions encompass cognitive processes like planning, organizing, initiating tasks, and more. They're vital for decision making, impulse control, pursuing goals, and adapting to various situations. Around 90% of people with ADHD are estimated to face executive function challenges.

2. The core executive functions are inhibition, working memory, and cognitive flexibility. These support a range of higher-level executive functions: planning, reasoning, problem solving, organizing, task initiation, decision making, time management, focusing, shifting attention, and goal-directed behavior.

3. Procrastination is rooted in our brain's evolutionary tendency to favor comfort and conserve energy. This survival mechanism, designed to keep us safe, hinders our pursuit of goals and tasks in modern times.

4. Most people have the misconception that they must wait for motivation to kick in before getting started on a task. However, the truth is that motivation doesn't precede action—it follows it. Beginning with some form of action is the catalyst for motivation.

5. Two simple cognitive strategies to reduce procrastination and make tasks feel less daunting are task breakdown and the body double technique.

6. To improve time management, break the habit of underestimating how long tasks may take. Using a timer for a few days helps to accurately measure the amount of time it takes to do something. Always allow extra time for any task or activity as a buffer for unforeseen events. To-do lists and calendars are vital daily tools for effective time management.

7. Techniques such as distractibility delay, workspace optimization, scheduling daily deep work blocks, avoiding multitasking, and setting boundaries with phone notifications can significantly enhance your work focus and productivity.

8. Working memory is affected by ADHD, but certain daily cognitive exercises like reverse order sequences, reverse spelling, memory card games, word list recall, and story retelling can help improve it.

9. You can optimize your learning skills by using techniques like the memory palace, association and visualization, chunking information, the Feynman technique, or by incorporating songs and rhymes.

10. Impulsive behavior is a common symptom of ADHD. A few mental techniques that you can use to reduce impulsive behavior are the stop signal technique, the response cost technique, mindfulness meditation, and cognitive training games.

5

HOW TO BUILD HEALTHY, LONG-LASTING HABITS

"I didn't let ADHD prevent me from achieving my goals, and neither should you."
— Howie Mandel, American actor and comedian

While habits play an important role in everyone's life, they're absolutely crucial for us as women with ADHD. Routines form the foundation on which daily life and long-term goals are built, offering structure in a world that would otherwise be chaotic. Habits create a framework to manage daily tasks and help reduce the mental effort required for making numerous small decisions. Completing daily chores becomes streamlined, freeing you from constant mental reminders.

When you repeat an action or a behavior for long enough that it becomes automatic, you create a habit. But the process of creating—and, even more importantly, sticking to—habits can be quite challenging when you're a woman with ADHD. Your executive functions like planning, organizing, shifting focus, and impulsive tendencies can complicate the habit-building process. Nevertheless, by acknowledging these challenges, we can tailor our approach to make habit formation feel less like an impossible mission. Building habits is doable, even with ADHD!

The Process of Habit Formation: How to Form Long-Lasting Habits

A habit is formed through the means of a continuous feedback loop: Cue > Craving > Response > Reward

1. **Cue Creation.** Building any habit will start with a cue or a trigger. A cue is a reminder that signals us into an action or routine, and it can be anything—a location, time, sound, etc. For example, going into the bathroom in the morning can serve as a location cue to start your morning routine.

2. **Craving.** A craving is the desire or motivation that follows the cue. It's the emotional or psychological response that makes you want to perform the habit. For example, once you wake up (cue), you might feel a craving to start your day feeling energized, which then motivates you to go out for a workout.

3. **Response.** The response is the action or behavior you engage in after experiencing the craving. For example, in response to the craving for energy, you have a 30-minute workout.

4. **Reward.** Our brains are designed to look for dopamine boosts and, therefore, crave rewards. A reward can be anything that brings a sense of satisfaction. Following the previous example, your reward is going to be an improved mood and energy boost due to a surge of endorphins after the workout.

Let's illustrate the habit formation process in action using another example—this time, a not-so-positive habit:

- **Cue:** feeling bored at work
- **Craving:** the desire for entertainment and distraction
- **Response:** opening your social media app and scrolling through posts
- **Reward:** feeling entertained and distracted from boredom

When repeating this for a long enough time, we create the habit of checking social media when bored. The more you repeat a habit loop, the stronger and more automatic it becomes. Similar to a well-trodden path becoming clearer with each step, every time you repeat an action in response to a cue, you strengthen specific neural pathways in your brain.

But how long does it actually take to form a habit? Research[1] suggests that, on average, it takes around 66 days for a habit to become automatic. However, this timeframe can range from 18 to over 200 days, depending on the complexity of the habit and individual differences.

How to Easily Implement Positive Habits

1. Learn what works for you, and choose something that you're more likely to enjoy.

You shouldn't build a habit just because you think you should or because others told you so. For a habit to stick for the long term, it needs to be in line with your values and likings. I'll give you a personal example: I wanted for so long to have some kind of workout routine in the morning, but the thought of going out for a run sounded absolutely dreadful. I never liked running, and despite several attempts, I couldn't sustain it as a long-term habit because I didn't enjoy it. So I had to find something that worked for me. Ultimately, I decided to include stretching and light exercises, like jumping rope, in my morning routine, and guess what? These actually stuck in my morning routine because I found them more enjoyable.

2. Start small and make the habits seem easy.

Because of the tendency to get easily overwhelmed, as a person with ADHD, you need to start small when trying to establish new habits. Begin by implementing one habit at a time, and if possible, break it down into more manageable chunks.

For instance, when I started working out in the morning, I made a deal with myself to start doing it for at least 10 minutes. It felt like an amount of time that was doable (even on those days when I didn't wake up particularly energetic), decreasing the likelihood of me feeling like I didn't want to do it.

So when you're looking to implement a new habit, ask yourself, "What is a reasonable amount of time that I can commit to this without feeling resistance?"

Remember, the feeling of resistance when thinking about performing a particular action is often a sign that the task is too big and should likely be broken down into smaller steps. Down the line, as a habit becomes ingrained into your routine, you can gradually increase its duration.

3. Connect a new habit to an old one.

An easy way to create a new habit and increase its chances of sticking for the long term is by linking it to an existing one. For instance, let's say that you want to develop the habit of reading daily. A great way to go about this is by linking it to your evening habit of getting into bed:

Cue: after getting into bed

Craving: the desire to relax, reduce screen time before sleep, and improve your knowledge

Response: spend 20 minutes reading a few pages from a book before bed

Reward: relaxation, reduced screen time before bed, and self-improvement through reading

By attaching the new habit of reading before sleep to the existing one of getting into your bed at night, you create a seamless transition between your bedtime action and reading practice.

4. Create environments that work *for* you and not *against* you.

Our surroundings significantly influence our behaviors, and for an ADHD woman striving to establish lasting habits, making environmental modifications is vital.

You'll need to create cues for the habits you want to integrate into your routine, as well as make the cues of unwanted habits less noticeable. For example, suppose that you're going to quit spending so much time on social media. In that case, you'll have to change your "digital environment" by removing the apps from your phone and therefore making access to them more difficult.

Here's another example: Let's say that you want to improve your eating habits and consume more fruits and veggies. Update your environment by placing a bowl of washed fruits on the kitchen counter. Conceal unhealthy snacks in less visible and accessible spots, and then gradually remove them completely from your home.

Do you want to be more productive during work? Identify potential distractions, such as phone notifications and clutter. Make sure that your workspace is organized, with everything you might need readily available so that unnecessary interruptions are avoided—put your phone on silent or in another room, keep a water glass next to you to quench your thirst without interrupting work, and declutter the room to minimize distractions.

So then, creating an environment that works *for* you and not *against* you involves:

- identifying the habit you want to establish or break
- analyzing your environment and assessing your surroundings to determine what cues are triggering (or potentially blocking) that habit
- placing visual cues related to that positive habit in prominent places
- hiding negative cues (items) associated with unwanted habits

During your journey of building lasting habits as a woman with ADHD, remember that Rome wasn't built in a day, and neither will habits that'll stand the test of time appear without a little bit of effort. The journey toward positive change requires the willingness to make improvements, as well as a patient attitude.

A desire to overhaul your entire routine in a short amount of time is natural, but remember that trying to change too much too fast is rather counterproductive. Instead, introduce or modify only one habit at a time. Allow it to settle into your routine before moving on to the next. Through dedicated effort, you'll gradually create habits that'll pave your way to more productive days, lowered stress levels, and a greater sense of achievement.

And finally, remember that because we live in a world that applauds constant hustle, it can be all too easy to feel inadequate when not constantly pushing ourselves. Your journey to success doesn't have to be a whirlwind of goals, and your routines don't need to rival an Olympic training regimen. It's about nurturing those few habits that'll bring the most improvement in your life and align with your priorities and values.

KEY TAKEAWAYS

1. Building healthy habits and routines provides a much-needed framework that helps us reduce mental effort on a daily basis and navigate our lives more effectively.

2. A habit is formed through the means of a continuous feedback loop: cue, craving, response, and reward.

3. As someone with ADHD, you need to keep in mind a few essential aspects that'll make implementing new habits easier: start small so that the new habits don't feel overwhelming; connect a new habit to an old one to increase the likelihood of it sticking long term; modify your environment so that it works *for* you and not *against* you; and choose habits that are in line with your likings, values, and priorities.

A quick break from our usual content. Before we dive back in, I want to ask you something...

If you had the chance to positively impact someone else's life — at no cost— would you do it?

Well, you have the opportunity right now.

You may have been on your ADHD journey for some time now, but I'm sure you can remember your first steps into it...

Do you remember feeling different, without knowing exactly why? Do you recall the shame and frustration of thinking you are lazy or scatterbrained? Back then you didn't know you had ADHD, and you blamed yourself. But now, you understand that it wasn't your fault.

Here's the thing: you could help another woman with ADHD stop blaming herself too. How? Simple! By leaving a review for this book and allowing her to discover this resource.

Give another woman with ADHD the opportunity to find the answers you wish you had earlier.

Your review, which doesn't cost anything, but a few seconds of your time, could change a fellow ADHD woman's life forever.

Simply scan the QR code below to leave your review:

Thank you so much for your help! Now back to our regularly scheduled content.

6

HOW TO BETTER ORGANIZE YOUR HOME

"Don't be afraid to ask for help, and to admit when you need it."
— Charles Schwab, American investor and financial executive

*H*ome organization is one of the main challenges we encounter as women with ADHD. Often, our impulsivity and difficulty in sustaining focus can lead to clutter buildup, misplaced items, and an overwhelming sense of chaos. Questions like, "Why is it so difficult to keep my home tidy?", "Why do I always have to struggle to find things when I need them?", or "Is it even possible for me to organize my home and not feel overwhelmed?" often echo in our minds.

I wholeheartedly understand the daily struggles of keeping home life in order. ADHD can make it hard to keep systems and routines in place for the long term. Nevertheless, even though the journey toward an organized home may sometimes appear overwhelming, employing the right strategies can effectively transform your living space. Below, I've shared the tips and techniques that have worked for me to better organize my home and life in general. Try them out to find which ones work best for you and are easiest to integrate into your routine.

The Power of Simplicity

The truth is that elaborate organizational systems are simply *not* for us, as ADHD can make the simplest tasks feel like climbing Mount Everest. Even seemingly straightforward tasks, like getting ready in the morning, can demand a monumental amount of energy and focus. Therefore, we need organizational systems that are straightforward, requiring minimal effort and brain power. Also, simply having fewer possessions makes household management much easier—the fewer items you have to juggle, the easier the home tidying process becomes.

> An effective organizational system or strategy for an ADHD person shouldn't aim for perfection but for practicality and long-term sustainability. Prioritizing functionality and ease of maintenance over aesthetics alone is key.

An efficient home tidying approach should seamlessly integrate into your routine, making tasks feel more manageable. The end goal isn't just a visually appealing living space but also one that empowers you to thrive without adding unnecessary stress and complexity.

I know very well that it's tempting to fall for those picture-perfect organizational systems that promise to transform your space into a magazine-worthy haven, but a pretty setup doesn't mean "practical" and "sustainable" for someone with ADHD. While it may look amazing initially, it can quickly become a source of frustration when it's time to put things back in their place. I speak from experience, as I've spent hours setting up complex shelving and storing, aiming for that perfect Pinterest look. But eventually, motivation would fizzle out, and I couldn't maintain things to the standards I'd initially set.

Do you know those posts on Instagram, the ones featuring a sock drawer where each pair is meticulously folded and arranged by color? They may be inspiring, but once you decide to use a similar setup, you might realize that the extra time and effort that goes into ensuring that every sock is folded just right is too much to handle. While visually appealing, it quickly becomes unsustainable to maintain this sort of routine. The time spent on such detailed organization starts to outweigh the convenience. It may look great on social media (as most things do), but sometimes, it just doesn't align with the practical needs of daily life.

Open shelves, for example, might not look as great as closed cabinets, but they'll be way more efficient since you can easily see everything placed on them. And, as a result, you won't have to expend too much energy to find what you need every single time you reach for something.

Simplicity and functionality should be the golden, guiding principles behind any organizational system for ADHD homes. This way, routines are streamlined and not hindered by unnecessary complexity. We want an organizing system that saves us time, mental effort, and stress. The simpler you can make it, the better!

Decluttering is the Way

The more stuff we accumulate, the harder it is to maintain order, so any organizing process should begin with decluttering. By limiting possessions and simplifying spaces, you not only clear clutter from your space but also from your mind. This is *so* valuable for our ADHD brains, since visual clutter can be particularly overwhelming.

But trying to overhaul and declutter a lot at once never works for someone with ADHD. I know this from personal experience, as I'd often start out determined and full of fire, pulling everything from the closets and cabinets, only to quickly feel overwhelmed and end up abandoning the mess.

It's best to start small—tackling one drawer or shelf at a time will feel (and is) more doable than conquering an entire room. Focusing on one small area until you completely finish it reduces the risk of leaving a job half-done and having mountains of clutter around the house. It not only helps prevent becoming overloaded but also allows you to see your progress clearly, which serves as motivating fuel. The sense of accomplishment from completing one area will give you the energy to move on to the next.

Additionally, when seeking motivation for decluttering, the body double technique can be incredibly useful. Enlisting your partner or another family member to clean with you will help you stay on track and motivate each other.

Common Excuses for Holding onto Unnecessary Items

While the ultimate goal is to create a peaceful, organized space where everything has its place, you might've noticed that when attempting to declutter, mental excuses can take over: "I might need this someday" or "My cousin might want this," for example. Especially when you have ample storage space, you don't see the harm in keeping these items for a little longer. However, a spacious house shouldn't be an excuse to accumulate excess belongings. Don't hold onto things you don't use just because space isn't an issue. You deserve a functional, peaceful home.

The only exceptions to this rule would be items that are tiny and take minimal space or those that are difficult to replace. But if something hasn't been used for a long time and can be easily repurchased, borrowed, or rented, it's time to let it go.

Another common mental excuse that may prevent us from parting with unnecessary items is thinking that we might be able to sell them. In reality, this often only prolongs the decision-making process and clutter. If you actually evaluate the time and effort involved in selling these unnecessary items and the small amount of money that could be earned, you'll often come to realize that it's simply not worth the trouble. So instead, consider donating unused items as a faster way to declutter. You'll be surprised at how little you miss the things that you've removed. And the reward of a clutter-free home will far outweigh the temporary discomfort.

The keep-donate-discard method is one of the simplest and most efficient ways to combat the clutter. Start out by dedicating three boxes or piles into which you'll categorize your items.

The "keep" box or pile is going to be for items you regularly use, genuinely love, and find essential. When considering whether to keep an item, simply ask yourself if it aligns with your current needs, lifestyle, and preferences. If the answer is yes, then it's a keeper.

Items that are in good condition but no longer serve you should go into the "donate" category. Include here everything from clothing, accessories, and gadgets to books that you've outgrown and haven't used in quite some time. Rather than letting these items gather dust, give them a new life by donating them to someone who'd appreciate and benefit from them. This way you free up space for yourself while making a positive impact on someone's life. It's an undeniable win-win.

Finally, the "discard" box or pile is for the items that are broken, worn out, expired, or no longer functional. They've served their purpose, and now they're just cluttering your space.

Employ this simple organizational method by focusing on one area at a time, whether it's a room, closet, or drawer. Avoid over-thinking it! Trust your instincts and go with your initial gut reaction, which is usually spot-on, to decide what to keep and what to throw.

In addition to the three categories—keep, donate and discard—there's also the category of sentimental items. These posses-sions may not have a practical purpose, but they hold a special place in our hearts, making them difficult to part with.

When it comes to these items, I'm all for setting limits on how much we get to keep. More specifically, I've found it helpful to designate a medium-sized box that can be easily stored. The rule is simple: If it fits inside the box, you can keep it. Anything that doesn't, should go. As a general guideline, try to limit your-self to keeping no more than two or three items that remind you of one particular place or person.

After completing the decluttering process, consider imple-menting the "one-in-one-out" strategy to prevent future clutter. This strategy involves letting go of an existing item, for every new item that enters your space. By doing so, you'll maintain control over the amount of possessions you own.

Avoid Impulsive Purchases

As ADHD women, we tend to engage in impulsive shopping quite often, and, unfortunately, the constant influx of new possessions can quickly pile up and create clutter all over again. To prevent this from happening, aim to shop more selectively and resist the urge to add things to your cart simply because they're on sale or seem interesting in that moment. Be intentional about what you bring into your home and life.

I know that this can be challenging at times. For this reason, it's crucial to introduce extra steps and friction into the buying process in order to curb those spontaneous purchases. For instance, remove stored payment information from your computer or phone, and avoid entering shops unless you genuinely need something (aimless browsing = danger!)

Extra Organizing Tips for a Tidy Home

We know that our organizing systems are efficient if we can easily find what we need and access any item's location without having to shuffle things around. I've shared below some extra organizing tips that have helped me along the way, and they should be able to help you, too:

1. **Make sure that the items you own take up less space than your storage allows.** Shelves and drawers should never be overcrowded, so the process of retrieving items and placing them back is effortless. If you have to move things around to get something from a shelf or drawer, it's a clear sign that the storage space is overcrowded.

People commonly assume they need additional storage space without first taking stock of their belongings and decluttering what's unnecessary. However, in most cases, merely reducing the amount of possessions is enough.

Additionally, using dividers and organizers for drawers and shelves is really helpful for storing items by category, allowing enough space to retrieve things without having to shuffle other stuff around.

2. Reduce duplicate items. While decluttering is about getting rid of things you no longer use, it's equally as important to consider how many items you have with the same function. Do you own 20 small bowls in your kitchen? Or five similar frying pans?

Keep them down to a reasonable amount so that you have enough cutlery and dishes for when you have a few friends and family members over, but not more than that.

3. Batch recurrent chores. Group tasks like cooking, doing groceries, or checking e-mails, to save time by handling them only once throughout your week or day.

For instance, I batch cook on Sundays, so I don't have to worry about food for the next few days. When it comes to e-mails, I allocate an hour in the afternoon to deal with them— this way I don't waste time during my work day and can focus on more important tasks.

4. Pair chores with a pleasant activity. Most chores can feel really mundane, so why not pair them with a more pleasurable activity, like listening to a podcast while scrubbing the bathroom or catching up with a friend over the phone while you tackle the laundry? This way, time will pass quickly, and you'll also have something enjoyable to focus on.

5. Handle it once. This rule is particularly helpful for managing mail. Once opened, if it serves no further purpose, promptly throw it away. However, if it's a bill to be paid or a letter requiring a reply, handle it on the spot if possible or place it in a "to deal with" pile. The same principle applies to digital mail. The goal is to prevent correspondence from being opened and left scattered, cluttering your space.

6. Establish a routine. While routines might feel tedious, they offer valuable mental peace and organization. Assign specific days for recurring chores—for instance, designate Saturday as laundry day or Friday for meal prep. As these activities become ingrained habits, home maintenance will become *so* much more manageable.

7. Clean a little each day. Besides maintaining an organized living space, tidying up a little every day helps make deep cleaning less daunting, saving you time and energy in the long run. Whether it's just 10 minutes tidying up a room, organizing a shelf, or simply discarding junk mail, these small efforts can significantly help maintain a neat living space.

8. Add it to your calendar. When a one-off project needs your attention, such as replacing a broken appliance or painting the hallway, schedule it in your calendar. This way, you don't forget about it and you also free up your mental space.

How to Stop Misplacing Your Belongings

Losing track of personal items is a frustrating, all too common struggle among many women with ADHD. Our easily distractible brains frequently misplace things amidst the whirl-wind of daily tasks, thoughts and other stimuli — all competing for our attention.

"Where did I put my keys?", and "Where is my phone? I liter-ally had it in my hand a minute ago!" Our belongings seem to vanish into thin air, mysteriously disappearing when we need them the most, leading us to tear apart the house in search of them.

While losing or misplacing things isn't strictly an ADHD experience, our attention span issues certainly exacerbate this problem. The good news is that by employing certain hacks and lifestyle adjustments, you can regain control. Vanished items and frantic mornings don't need to define your existence!

One of the simplest and most effective hacks to prevent misplacing your items entails assigning a designated home to every single thing you own—hang keys by the door, place bills in their dedicated spot within the office inbox, return clothes to their designated wardrobe sections, and so on. Everything should always have a precise location to return to.

> It's essential to cultivate the habit of not unloading important items from your hands unless it's to their designated place in your purse, car, home, and so on.

At first, consistently returning items to their assigned spots will likely be challenging. Our ADHD brain craves instant gratification, tempting us to just set things down wherever. But I've come to realize that investing a few extra seconds to return an item to its designated place actually saves a significant amount of time, frustration and mental effort in the long run. Eventually, this process (whilst dreadful at first!) becomes instinctive. And what could be more beneficial for a busy, distracted brain than autopilot organization to prevent losing and misplacing items?

Another effective strategy to help you keep better track of your belongings involves clearly labeling storage spaces in your home, such as "sock drawer" or "personal documents shelf". This practice helps build associations in your brain between objects and their designated spots, and therefore making it easier to retrieve items. Additionally, it prevents the formation of those dreaded junk drawers filled with miscellaneous items and spares you from the constant mental effort of having to figure out where everything belongs.

Lastly, consider attaching digital trackers to important personal items like phones, keys, and wallets to easily locate them at all times and spare yourself from the unnecessary stress of having to search (and shout!) for them.

KEY TAKEAWAYS:

1. An effective organizational system for an ADHD woman shouldn't strive for perfection but rather for practicality and long-term sustainability. The primary goal is functionality and ease of upkeep—not aesthetics.

2. Start with small spaces when decluttering to prevent overwhelm and to get a sense of reward much quicker. The body double technique can be immensely helpful for staying on track and maintaining motivation during home organization.

3. We often find excuses to keep items we no longer use, but these only prolong the clutter. The keep-donate-discard method is a very efficient strategy for decluttering.

4. To prevent the number of possessions from getting out of control again after you've decluttered, implement the one-in-one-out strategy: for each new item you bring home, you let go of an existing one.

5. To prevent impulsive purchases, create friction in the purchase process by removing stored info from your devices. Also, go to shops only when you need something—not simply to browse.

6. To prevent losing or misplacing your belongings, assign a designated home to every single thing you own. Label storage spaces in your home to stay organized, avoid clutter, and reduce the stress of searching for misplaced items. Additionally, consider using digital trackers to monitor your essential personal belongings.

7

HOW TO NAVIGATE SOCIAL LIFE & ROMANCE

"The hardest challenge is to be yourself in a world where everyone else is trying to make you somebody else."
— E.E. Cummings, American poet

Managing Your Social Life

*E*ver felt overwhelmed trying to juggle multiple social commitments? Or like you're just "not good" at friendships? Sometimes it seems that no matter how much we'd like to be social, we often end up disappointing friends due to our tendency to cancel plans at the last minute, space out during conversations, or forget birthdays and other important events.

ADHD symptoms can make it difficult to maintain an active social life. But once you start recognizing the areas where you struggle the most, you can begin taking steps to work on them.

Some of the most common social challenges specific to people with ADHD are:

- Problems following through on plans
- The tendency to hyperfocus on work or hobbies and neglect friends
- Impulsively overcommitting to events
- Frequently interrupting or talking over others
- Forgetting about friends' birthdays and other important details
- Social anxiety, which leads to avoidance of group events

According to studies, social anxiety disorder (SAD) is one of the most common comorbid conditions of ADHD (Kessler et al., 2006). The causal factors for this include executive function deficits, communication difficulties, low self-esteem, rejection sensitivity, and emotional dysregulation. Moreover, there are many overlapping symptoms between ADHD and social anxiety disorder that can contribute to misdiagnosis, including:

1. **Difficulty concentrating in social situations.** Both ADHD and social anxiety can lead to problems in maintaining focus during social interactions. With ADHD, this is mostly due to a wandering mind and impulsivity, while with social anxiety, it's due to excessive worry about how one is perceived.

2. **Restlessness or avoidance in social settings.** Individuals with ADHD may find themselves fidgety or unable to sit still in social situations, while those with social anxiety may seek to avoid these situations altogether due to intense feelings of fear of embarrassment.

3. **Difficulty initiating or sustaining conversations.** Both conditions can impact social skills. ADHD people struggle with distractibility, being overly talkative, impulsively interrupting conversations, and missing out on social cues. In contrast, those with social anxiety might avoid initiating conversations due to

trouble with making eye contact and a fear of saying the wrong thing and being judged for it.

4. Performance anxiety. Both ADHD and SAD can lead to this common form of anxiety. People with ADHD might worry about performing well in social situations, while those with social anxiety may dread public speaking or being the center of attention.

5. Low self-esteem. Both conditions contribute to low levels of confidence and self-worth. Individuals with ADHD might struggle with the perception that they're different or not able to meet expectations. At the same time, social anxiety can lead to a negative self-image due to perceived failures in social interactions.

Due to all of these overlapping symptoms, SAD often remains undiagnosed in those who also carry the weight of ADHD. This is why a thorough evaluation by a qualified clinician is essential, as it can untangle the thread of symptoms and provide much-needed clarity.

Developing Social Skills

Social skills are like a toolbox that equips us to navigate the world of social interactions and connections. This encompassing term—"social skills"—embraces a range of abilities that empower individuals to communicate effectively and engage with others:

- **Active listening skills.** This is the art of not just hearing words but truly understanding the messages, emotions, and intentions behind them. It involves giving attention and responding thoughtfully.

- **Verbal and non-verbal communication skills.** These are the keys to expressing yourself clearly and accurately. Verbal communication involves words and language, while non-verbal cues like facial expressions and gestures add depth to your messages.
- **Interpersonal skills.** These qualities include empathy, understanding others' viewpoints, and building connections based on trust and mutual respect. They help nurture healthy relationships.
- **Assertiveness skills.** The ability to act in an assertive way empowers someone to communicate confidently and effectively. Assertiveness allows people to express their needs and opinions while respecting others.
- **Conflict management skills.** These abilities allow us to address disagreements in a constructive manner. It involves listening, finding common ground, and working toward resolutions that benefit all parties.
- **Persuasion skills.** Essentially, persuasion is the knack of influencing others' thoughts and actions through compelling communication. It requires understanding their needs and presenting your perspective effectively.

For those seeking to enhance their social skills, below are a few tips that can help pave the way for more effective interactions and meaningful connections.

1. **Practice being fully present in conversations.** Absorb both verbal and non-verbal cues, and ask thoughtful questions that show your interest and help you stay engaged. When receiving criticism, listen attentively and ask for clarifications if needed to understand the feedback fully. Try to remain open to constructive criticism and avoid defensive reactions. Remember that social competence, like any other skill, thrives on practice.

2. Strive for balanced and reciprocal conversations. Share your thoughts while also giving space for others to contribute. Staying on topic helps keep the flow of conversation engaging and focused.

3. Educate your friends about ADHD traits. Don't shy away from discussing your ADHD traits that might affect your social interactions. Open and honest conversations about your unique strengths and challenges can foster understanding and empathy among friends and acquaintances.

4. Create comfort zones. Design your social environments to suit your needs. Choose quieter settings if noise is distracting, or opt for smaller gatherings where you can engage more deeply and not feel overwhelmed by a large crowd. Also, regularly schedule one-on-one time with close friends that allows you to engage in deeper conversations and establish more meaningful bonds.

5. Join supportive communities and groups. These offer a safe space where you can get encouragement, share your experiences, and gain understanding. If the idea of joining an in-person support group feels overwhelming due to social anxiety, you can consider online groups, which also provide a safe space where you can connect with others walking a similar path. Participating in discussions, sharing stories, and seeking advice from the comfort of your own space allows you to slowly become more accustomed to social interaction.

6. Ease into socializing. Just as you wouldn't sprint a marathon, gradually increase your exposure to social situations at a pace that feels comfortable.

7. Seek professional support. Don't hesitate to reach out for guidance from professionals who specialize in ADHD and social skills. Psychologists and ADHD coaches can provide tailored strategies, constructive feedback, and a structured approach to enhancing your social competence. If you've been working independently on improving your social skills but find that certain situations still trigger anxiety and uncertainty, it's okay to recognize that you might need more guidance. Through sessions, you learn strategies to manage social anxiety and navigate conversations with more confidence.

CBT Techniques to Manage Social Anxiety

1. **Cognitive restructuring** involves identifying anxious automatic thoughts, challenging them by considering contrary evidence, and replacing them with more balanced thoughts.

- Identify anxious automatic thoughts that may arise in social situations.

Example: "I worry that if I attend this work event, everyone will get to know me better and might start thinking that I'm weird."

- Challenge these thoughts by considering the evidence against them.

Example: "My friends enjoy my company, so maybe I'm not as strange as I think."

- Replace these thoughts with more balanced ones.

Example: "Even if I mess up, people usually don't judge me as harshly as my anxiety may lead me to believe."

2. **Exposure therapy** involves gradually facing situations that trigger anxiety in order to build tolerance and reduce fear.

- Create a hierarchy of anxiety-provoking social situations from least to most distressing. (e.g., making a phone call, attending a social event, etc.)

- Begin exposing yourself to these situations. Start with the least anxiety-inducing situation and work your way up. Resist avoiding or escaping. The initial peak of anxiety when starting the process will eventually decrease as you become more accustomed to exposing yourself to these situations.
- Stay present during exposure and focus on your breath. Observe your thoughts without judgment.
- Be patient. Spend enough time in the exposure situation to notice your anxiety decreasing.
- Practice the same situation multiple times until the anxiety decreases significantly. Then go on to the next situation in your hierarchy that's slightly more challenging, and repeat this process.

Relaxation techniques, like deep breathing, mindfulness, and positive self-talk, can be used before entering these social situations to help you stay grounded and composed, as well as to reduce anxiety. Also, consider seeking professional guidance for this method, as exposure therapy can be more effective with a trained therapist who can guide you and support you through the process.

3. Social skills training involves exposing yourself to safe social situations that will gradually help strengthen your abilities to adapt and thrive in social settings.

- Watch videos modeling proper social skills like conversing, listening, and asserting needs.
- Roleplay scenarios with a friend or your therapist, practicing these skills.
- Put these skills into practice in real-life situations and, if possible, get feedback from trusted friends afterward.

Managing Romantic Relationships

Dating and romantic relationships are never easy, but they can be especially tricky when afflicted with ADHD. Impulsiveness can often lead to making reckless choices, restlessness results in difficulty maintaining long-term relationships, and forgetfulness, mood swings, and disorganization can strain bonds with partners. On top of that, social anxiety makes it hard to meet someone in the first place!

Taking the time to observe and become aware of your specific ADHD difficulties is the first step in the process. With this awareness in mind, I'd like to share with you a few valuable tips that have helped me and that can guide you as well in navigating romance more easily and creating stronger bonds in your relationships.

Openly communicate with your partner about your ADHD. Explaining how your condition affects you and your relationship is essential, as honest conversations help build trust and stronger bonds. Make sure that these discussions take the form of two-way dialogues and not one-sided lectures. Explain your specific ADHD symptoms, and use situational examples of how these manifest for you. Share how ADHD impacts your relationship, the fact that you might need reminders, or that you might be more emotionally sensitive because of it. Also, make sure that you ask your partner to share their perspective on how they think ADHD affects the relationship. Come prepared with some solutions that'll help manage these problems, showing that you're committed to mitigating impact. Reassure your partner that you're not using your ADHD as an excuse for hurtful behaviors—rather, you're taking responsibility for your actions but want to work on them as a team. Ensure to frame things positively whenever you can. While ADHD can make relationships uniquely challenging, it also provides an opportunity for growth together.

Change can't happen overnight, and so ongoing open communication is key for this positive change to happen. Thank your partner for their willingness to learn about ADHD. Express your appreciation for their grace and understanding as you figure things out together. The more your partner knows how ADHD influences you, the more support and patience they can offer.

Schedule date nights or quality time together. Consistent one-on-one time without distractions is crucial—just make sure that you add these dates to your calendar so that they don't slip through the cracks. Also, before big events like anniversaries or holidays, set up reminders on your phone to go off long enough in advance so you have time to prepare.

Try new activities together. Try activities that align with your ADHD brain's thirst for novelty—take a couples' cooking class, go on a hiking adventure, or try out a new restaurant that has opened in your city. Seek out the kind of experiences that engage you both.

Develop a system for managing and dividing up chores. The key here is to devise this in accordance with each of your strengths. And, as with anything else, clear expectations and organization reduce conflicts.

Make sure that you speak each other's love language. Find out the best ways that show your partner how loved they are and make those gestures more often.

Now, for my lovely ADHD ladies out there who are still single but ready to mingle, I have a few strategies that can help ease the social anxiety around dating. To start with, trying online dating can be a fantastic baby step to put yourself out there in case you struggle with meeting people in person. Browse some apps to find the ones that align with your interests and values, craft your profile to showcase your personality, and remember —there's no pressure to meet with people face to face if you're not feeling it. Simply testing the waters and chatting with matches is a safe way to start overcoming social anxiety.

If you feel more comfortable starting potential romantic relationships as friends first, you could join some meetup groups centered around some of the activities you enjoy. This is a fabulous way to organically get to know people. You can even ask trusted friends to introduce you to their single friends so that you don't have the pressure of a formal blind date.

Prior to any in-person dates, consider preparing some go-to conversation topics so that you don't feel tongue-tied. Remember that your date is most likely just as nervous and concerned about how they come across as you are. They're most probably not judging you as harshly as you might anticipate!

After your dates, write down what you think went well, and potentially one or two things that you'd want to improve next time instead of obsessively dwelling on awkward moments.

A final aspect worth mentioning is that impulsiveness can go hand in hand with poor decision making when it comes to dating, and it can manifest, among many other things, as risky sexual behavior. While the thrill of new casual relationships may be irresistible to your ADHD brain that craves stimulation, don't downplay the long-term consequences in favor of some instant gratification. To avoid putting yourself in these situations in the first place, avoid any substances like drugs and alcohol that lower inhibitions. Take it slowly when dating to build trust before intimacy and not get swept up in the moment. Lastly, if nothing else works, consider seeking counseling to get to the root of what motivates your urges for risky behavior and learn to develop healthier coping outlets. The key here is to be self-aware and proactive—don't wait for problems to happen. With support and strategies, you can make choices that satisfy your ADHD cravings for excitement while also protecting your mental and physical health.

KEY TAKEAWAYS:

1. ADHD-specific executive function challenges can bring certain difficulties to our social lives. Things like spacing out during conversations or forgetting about plans and friends' birthdays can often make us feel like we're not very good at navigating the social aspects of life.

2. Social anxiety disorder (SAD) is very common among people with ADHD. The many overlapping symptoms between ADHD and SAD can often contribute to misdiagnosis.

3. The first step to better social skills is self-awareness about the specific areas that we need to work on. Improving listening skills, becoming more present in conversations, creating suitable social environments, joining supportive groups, educating friends about ADHD traits, and seeking professional guidance can help us better navigate social life.

4. CBT techniques, like cognitive restructuring, exposure therapy, and social skills training, can help manage and significantly improve social anxiety symptoms.

5. Many ADHD symptoms, including impulsiveness, forgetfulness, mood swings, and organizational issues, can make the entire process of dating and maintaining romantic relationships more difficult than it already is.

6. Open communication with your partner about how your ADHD affects you is essential.

7. Single women with ADHD who also struggle with social anxiety can ease dating fears by starting with online dating. Engaging in conversations online can help gradually build confidence. Preparing conversation topics prior to in-person dates can help alleviate anxiety. After each date, focusing on improvements rather than awkward moments helps build social confidence and comfort.

8. ADHD-related impulsiveness can lead to risky behaviors when dating. Therefore, try to avoid substances that lower inhibitions, and take time to build trust before intimacy to prevent negative consequences. If needed, consider counseling in order to address any motivators for risky behavior and to develop healthier coping mechanisms.

8

HOW TO NAVIGATE WORK & CAREER

"The truth is, there is no such thing as 'normal'; there are just a series of spectrums on which we all fall, and how normal we are is largely determined by how well our strengths and weaknesses match the social norms of the times we live in."
— Unknown

ooking back at the time before my diagnosis, I can see so many ADHD symptoms surfacing in my professional life. I struggled to stay engaged in tasks for long periods, needed frequent breaks, and regularly ended up working late because the office noise hindered my daytime productivity with everyone else around. I struggled to prioritize tasks, and so I ended up missing deadlines often. My mind would wander during most meetings, causing me to forget crucial details that were being discussed. Plus, once the excitement of a new job wore off, I would start dreading it so badly that all I wanted was to find a new job.

Back then, I didn't realize that these were actually signs of ADHD. At the time, I just thought it was me functioning differently, not being a very productive, consistent, and smart individual. Not for one second did I consider that these things were due to a different brain wiring. It would've made a world of difference if I'd known the real cause of my behavior years earlier. But since I couldn't go back in time, the next best thing was to write a book about my experience so that others could learn from it and, ultimately, avoid so much hardship.

Many ADHD women struggle in one way or another—changing jobs frequently, having difficulty making workplace friendships, being late for work often, not being able to maintain focus for long, and a general lack of progress in their careers.

A diagnosis can be so helpful and so freeing because it can finally explain all that we experience. We realize that we're not broken humans, bad employees, or professionals incapable of success. And once we have this awareness, we can start looking for solutions.

That said, it's important to know that while ADHD brings its fair share of challenges in the workplace, it doesn't mean that you won't be able to have a fulfilling career or find positions that play to your strengths. In the following pages, we'll delve deeper into some common workplace challenges that most women with ADHD face and explore strategies for addressing them.

1. Handling Time Management

While we've already explored ADHD-specific time management challenges and introduced a few strategies to improve this area in your life back in Chapter 4, in this section you'll be provided with a few additional tips particularly relevant to your daily work routine. (Many of these suggestions will apply to those of you in an office setting, but even if that's not you, plenty of these tips can still be adapted to your situation.)

- Use timers and alerts to switch tasks. Got a 1 p.m. meeting? Set a 12:45 reminder that gives you enough time to wrap up your current assignment and prepare for it.
- Assign each task a time frame.
- Schedule reminders leading up to deadlines.
- Block your calendar to establish periods of focused work. For instance, implement a "No Meetings" rule between 9 a.m. and 12 p.m., and designate that time as your deep work time.
- Break down complex projects into actionable steps with due dates.
- Reward your progress by celebrating milestones along the way to help maintain motivation.
- Be as realistic as possible when planning your schedule to avoid overwhelming yourself. Allocate some buffer time for each task.

2. Memory Management

Memory difficulties in the workplace can be particularly taxing, both to our self-esteem and our career progress. Here are some tips on how we can stay proactive:

- Take detailed notes or, if possible, use recording devices to retain crucial information in meetings. If you can, delegate this task and ask for written summaries after meetings to solidify the next steps.
- Use acronyms and acrostics for remembering key information.

- For each project, create a checklist to help you stay focused and organized. Ensure that you keep it visible —on your desktop, whiteboard, or another easily accessible location.
- Set reminders and alerts in your calendar for everything, from appointments to deadlines and daily tasks.
- Use a daily planner religiously to keep track of your to-do list. Refer to it frequently.
- Employ sticky notes as visual reminders in your workspace for essential tasks.
- Minimize physical and digital clutter—keeping a clean desk and inbox can make a big difference in your distractibility.
- Repeat or summarize important details to help solidify them in your memory.

3. Handling Impulsiveness

- When dealing with frustrating e-mails, take a moment before replying. Draft your response, step away for about 10 minutes, and then return to review your response before hitting send.
- If someone becomes heated in a conversation, consider revisiting the topic once you've both had the chance to cool down.
- If possible, have a mentor at work or a trustworthy work friend observe you in meetings and provide feedback afterward. Another option would be to work with a coach to practice appropriate responses to frustrating situations.
- Integrate relaxation and meditation techniques into your daily routine. Practice deep breathing when you feel irritation building up.

4. Staying Focused

- Keep a notebook handy to write down sudden ideas without derailing your current work.
- Reduce the frequency of e-mail check-ins by designating a specific time, such as one hour in the afternoon for this task, instead of constantly checking them throughout the day.
- Use focus apps that block distracting websites during work sprints.
- When you need to focus deeply on certain tasks, escape into an empty conference room to minimize interruptions.
- Invest in some noise-canceling headphones to block out distractions.
- If office noise becomes overwhelming, try working on the more important projects during quieter hours. If the possibility exists, work from home or request to use a more tranquil workspace.
- Take regular five to 10-minute breaks to stretch and reset.
- Prepare talking points before meetings to stay focused and avoid going off-topic.

5. Getting Organized

- Make master checklists for big projects and break them down into manageable steps.
- Purge e-mails and documents regularly—for instance, every Friday before leaving work.
- Designate specific homes for every item on your desk, from stationery to important documents.

6. Managing Hyperactivity

- Incorporate regular movement breaks into your routine. Go for a quick walk, make a cup of tea, or stretch for a few minutes throughout your day.
- Keep some fidget toys on hand, like a stress ball, to help with those moments of restlessness.
- Use stability balls or standing desks in your workplace to promote active work.
- Consider transitioning to more active roles that involve stimulating and diverse responsibilities while minimizing routine tasks.

7. Improving Interpersonal Skills in Your Workplace

- Be aware of your body language and tone, as a smile and an open posture can make a significant difference in how people respond to you.
- Offer compliments to acknowledge others' ideas and to show that you're a team player.
- After any tense exchanges with co-workers, follow up to smooth things over. This will go a long way in maintaining positive working relationships.
- Engage in roleplaying scenarios with a friend or your therapist to practice appropriate interactions.

Should You Disclose Your ADHD?

Deciding whether to inform your employer about your ADHD is a personal choice. It's not absolutely necessary to disclose it, and you may opt not to do so, especially if you're performing well in your job and don't need any accommodations from your management. Because the truth is that whether we like it or not, there's still a stigma around ADHD, and many still consider it "not a real disability." So if you feel that disclosing your ADHD might cause your colleagues or supervisor to discriminate against you, it should be a good enough reason not to do it. However, if your job may be at risk without certain accommodations from your employer, it only makes sense to disclose your ADHD so that you have everything you need to succeed in your role.

Also, keep in mind that you can request accommodations without having to disclose your ADHD. First, you could devise your own accommodations, like coming in early, taking work home, or using some of the coping strategies from the previous section. Second, you could frame your requests from a position of strength instead of mentioning the disability itself.

For example, instead of saying, "I have ADHD, which makes it really hard for me to focus with all the noise and activity in the office," you could say, "I've noticed that I'm significantly more productive when working from home where I don't have as many distractions. Would it be possible to work remotely two days a week so that I can concentrate better on my tasks?"

Rather than saying, "My ADHD makes it impossible for me to remember all the steps in this complicated procedure. I need written checklists," go with something like, "I want to do the best job possible on these intricate procedures. It would help me ensure that no step is missed if I could reference a checklist for complex tasks. Could we implement some standard check-lists for certain processes?"

Or instead of saying, "I need you to be more understanding when it comes to deadlines because my ADHD makes it hard to manage my time well," try something like, "I'd like to discuss ways in which I can strengthen my time management skills. For instance, breaking large assignments into smaller milestones on my calendar has really helped me improve recently. Do you have other recommendations so that I can continue getting deliverables in on time?"

The focus should always be on tangible solutions—not on excuses. Frame requests around optimizing your performance and contributions. It'll make accommodation needs seem less like special treatment and more like removing obstacles so that you can truly excel.

If you eventually decide to take the full disclosure path because you need more complex accommodations in order to succeed, consider these tips:

- Make sure that you pick a private time to have the discussion, like asking to speak in your boss's office. Frame it as positive: "I'd like to share something that'll allow me to contribute better."
- Educate your manager on ADHD symptoms and explain how they specifically affect your work performance. Give examples of challenges and successes.
- Emphasize the discussion on the steps you're already taking to manage your symptoms and ask for their support with additional accommodations. "It would really help me to be able to use noise-canceling headphones."
- Present solutions and be open to problem solving together. You want to come across as self-aware and committed to handling your ADHD proactively.
- Know your rights. The ADA (Americans with Disabilities Act) protects employees with disabilities and requires employers to make reasonable accommodations.
- While disability discrimination is illegal, you need to be prepared for the possibility that you'll face stigma

regardless. If faced with ignorance, stay calm and use it as a teaching moment, or direct these people to ADHD organizations.

Disclosing your ADHD, as I've mentioned, is a personal choice. Take your time to assess the risks and benefits of bringing it up in your workplace before doing so.

I always recommend positioning requests in terms of performance needs, as mentioned in the examples above, rather than disability status wherever possible. With the right framing at the right time and place, you should be able to obtain the support you need while minimizing the potential downsides of disclosure.

Qualities of ADHD in the Workplace

It's important to account for the fact that ADHD doesn't bring only challenges to the workplace—there are also many positive qualities. We're so used to hearing that ADHD makes our working life a struggle, but there's plenty of good stuff that it brings to our jobs.

- **Out-of-the-box thinking.** Our different brain wiring gives us the advantage of creativity and innovation. For instance, in my past jobs, I was the person who always came up with original solutions and ideas. Having a non-conventional perspective pays off tremendously in creative roles like marketing, for example, that require fresh and innovative thinking.
- **Hyperfocus.** Our moments of hyperfocus can be a huge asset. When engaged in a project we care deeply about, we'll work tirelessly for hours. ADHD might often mean a distractible mind, but when we're deeply

engrossed in something, we're a productivity powerhouse.

- **Resilience.** Most of us have likely faced countless challenges and setbacks due to ADHD, which have most certainly toughened us up. In the workplace, this resilience can be a real strength, especially during high-pressure situations.
- **Heightened intuition.** A knack for spotting details that others often miss is also part of the ADHD package. This unique skill can make you a valuable problem solver as well as an asset when it comes to quality control.
- **Empathy.** This quality helps us greatly connect with others on a more profound level. In the workplace, it helps us show some of our colleagues support and understanding like no one else can. People appreciate having a compassionate ear, and empathy can help you excel in roles that involve teamwork and communication.
- **Ability to "bring the fun."** Let's not forget that our ADHD generally makes it easy for us to liven up mundane tasks and lighten the mood in an otherwise stodgy and perhaps boring workday.

So next time you feel discouraged, and perhaps focus too much on the negatives of your neurodivergent brain, remember all these qualities and the tremendous potential you have. ADHD does bring its challenges and quirks, but it also encompasses many strengths that can set you apart in the professional world. Most importantly, if you haven't already, seek out roles that bring these qualities to the surface and make the ADHD short-comings less visible.

KEY TAKEAWAYS:

1. While ADHD brings its fair share of challenges in the workplace, it doesn't mean that you can't be successful in your career. Finding the right behavioral coping techniques and strategies is essential to cover those areas that you particularly struggle with.

2. Deciding whether to disclose your ADHD diagnosis to your employer is a personal choice. It's important to assess the benefits and risks of your specific situation before making a decision in this regard. Remember that if you need certain accommodations at work, it's not necessary to disclose your diagnosis—you can simply ask for these by framing them as performance needs.

3. While it's easy to think that ADHD only brings challenges in the workplace, the reality is that ADHD also brings many awesome qualities, such as attention to detail, creativity, out-of-the-box thinking, strong problem-solving skills, resilience, the ability to make tedious tasks fun, hyperfocus, and empathy.

9

HOW TO BETTER MANAGE YOUR FINANCES

"Everybody is a genius. But if you judge a fish by its ability to climb a tree, it will live its whole life believing it is stupid."
— Albert Einstein

udgeting, paying bills on time, and planning finances for the future can feel wildly daunting for many women with ADHD. Poor organization, time blindness, and impulse spending sabotage our best financial intentions, leaving us feeling ashamed and inadequate. And constantly avoiding financial matters only worsens the situation.

The good news is that any ADHD woman can establish healthier money habits with a little bit of willingness and practice.

In this chapter, we'll examine common ADHD-related financial challenges and explore solutions for them, including budgeting, bill payments, paperwork organization, debt reduction, and long-term planning. It's time to feel empowered instead of overwhelmed when dealing with money!

Impulsivity and Overspending

As we all know too well, a core ADHD trait is poor impulse control. In a financial context, this can manifest when, for instance, you spot something you want in a store, and the impulse to purchase takes over without you fully considering the financial consequences. This longing for instant gratification can lead to overspending when you don't pause to reflect on whether the purchase is truly needed or even affordable.

To curb these impulse buys, below are some ideas for you to consider implementing:

- Delete your credit card information from regularly used online marketplaces, like Amazon. Having to fetch your wallet and manually enter the card number provides your brain with some extra time to reconsider the purchase.
- For larger buys (for example, anything over $100), make it a mandatory rule to pause and "sleep on it" for at least 24 hours before proceeding. The waiting period often allows the initial impulse to fade.
- Make a list of discretionary wants and revisit it later when the immediate craving is diminished.
- When you do indulge in small impulse purchases, hold yourself accountable by tracking the money spent on these in your budget. Keeping a record will help to curb your future urges.

The goal here isn't to deprive yourself of any purchase that would bring you joy but rather to make your buying purchases more intentional.

Disorganization and Expense Tracking

When it comes to organizing finances, establishing a streamlined and structured approach for your money is crucial to reducing money management chaos. Here are a few ideas for you to consider implementing:

- Choose a system that fits your preferences in order to keep tabs on your balance. Whether it's a paper planner, a budgeting app, or spreadsheets, avoid forcing yourself into a one-size-fits-all method that doesn't resonate with you. As the saying goes, what doesn't click won't stick!
- Dedicate some time each week to review your finances. For example, set aside an hour every Saturday to check all your accounts, track your expenses from the past week, and ensure that bills are covered.
- Use digital calendar alerts to remind you to check accounts and other financial tasks. These notifications will help you stay on track between your scheduled financial check-ins.

Avoiding, Procrastinating, or Forgetting to Pay Bills

ADHD-related executive function challenges often lead to procrastination with routine tasks like paying bills. This avoidance generally stems from the aversion to tedious administrative tasks. However, late payments may potentially harm your credit score, in addition to the unnecessary fees. To prevent this from happening, consider implementing the following suggestions:

- Set up automatic payments for any recurring bills, like rent and utilities, to minimize the need for manual money movements and reduce the risk of forgetting about some of them.
- Use calendar reminders for bills requiring manual payment.
- If you've struggled with paying bills on time throughout your life, consider rewarding yourself every time you manage to pay a bill promptly. Treat yourself to small rewards, like a nice meal at your favorite restaurant, your favorite beverage, or watching an episode of a TV series you enjoy. This positive reinforcement will help you build consistency.

Misplacing Documents

Constantly searching for misplaced financial documents is another common issue for ADHD brains. To prevent the frustration and panic that can arise from not finding important documents, consider the following tips:

- Always create digital backups of essential documents. Scan or take photos of important hard copy paperwork and save them in a cloud or on an external hard drive.
- Use folder labels and dividers to neatly organize your paperwork and to make retrieval quick and efficient.
- Designate a home for important documents. Choose a physical location, like a filing cabinet, drawer, or box, for storing all your financial documentation. Avoid scattering documents across different locations, and

make it a habit to return documents to their assigned spot after each use.

Racking Up Large Credit Card Balances

Swiping that little piece of plastic can make it easy to overspend without a full appreciation of the financial consequences. To improve your credit card usage, consider putting these suggestions into practice:

- Only use credit cards if you have the cash to pay off the balance in full each month to avoid interest charges. Learn to treat your credit cards the same as your debit cards.
- Consider lowering your credit limits if you notice your balances creeping up. Having less credit available will make it harder for you to overspend!
- Monitor your credit card statements closely each month. Daily spending apps can help you keep track of your balance in real time.
- Leave your credit cards at home to avoid the temptation of impulse purchases.
- If you've already accumulated high credit card debt that you can't pay off all at once, set up auto payments for at least the minimum amount due each month so that you never miss a payment. And, whenever possible, pay more than the monthly minimum to make quicker progress.
- Credit cards can either be your best friend or your worst enemy when it comes to building credit. If you're worried about overspending, start using a secured credit card. These cards require a deposit that acts as your credit limit, making them less risky for impulsive spending. Once you become comfortable using credit

cards responsibly, you can consider transitioning to an unsecured card with a low spending limit.

- Your credit utilization ratio, which is the percentage of your credit limit that you actually use, plays a big role in your credit score. Aim to keep it below 30%. For instance, if you have a credit limit of $1000, you should aim to limit your spending to $300.
- Be wary of retail store cards. While they might be tempting with their discounts, they often have high interest rates. Be cautious about opening too many of these, as they can negatively affect your credit score!
- Speaking of your credit score, keep a close watch on it —as well as your credit reports. There are various free apps and websites that provide monthly updates. Regular monitoring helps you spot and correct any errors and track your progress.

Trouble With Saving for the Future

ADHD challenges, particularly struggling with delayed gratification, can make it hard to prioritize future savings over satisfying immediate desires. But we all know that saving is essential in order to achieve financial stability and reach long-term goals like creating a retirement fund or buying a home. Here are some practical tips to help you become a more effective saver:

- Pay yourself first. Automate transferring a portion of each paycheck into a savings account. Ideally, you should aim to save around 20% of your paycheck, but if that feels too much for you, it's perfectly okay to start with 10%. Initially, the most important thing is getting into the habit of saving regularly rather than the amount saved each month. Just set up autopay and then forget about it. That way, your money is stashed away before you're tempted to spend it on impulse buys.

- Give your savings a clear purpose by naming your savings accounts based on your specific goals. For instance, you could call one "house deposit fund." This small change makes the entire saving process feel more real and motivating. Also, adding snapshots of your goal to the savings account app, like the house you want or your ideal vacation, can help reinforce why you're saving.
- Celebrate savings milestones. Whenever you hit a savings goal, treat yourself to a little celebration. It'll feel good and will also give you a boost to keep going!
- Place your savings into harder-to-access accounts so that you won't be tempted to dip into them for everyday stuff.

Budgeting Fundamentals

Budgeting and managing finances can be a challenge for many of us ADHDers, but these aspects shouldn't feel complicated at all. As long as you follow a few basic money management rules, you should be able to do just fine.

First, it's essential to divide your income keeping in mind the 50/30/20 rule, meaning that you should:

- **Allocate 50% of your income to cover essential needs.** This refers to rent or mortgage, transportation, groceries, utilities, and any other necessary expenses that you require for a basic standard of living. The less you spend on this section, the more you can put toward other priorities.

- **Dedicate 30% of your income to the "wants" category.** This percentage includes everything you might want to purchase that isn't a must— entertainment, clothing, eating out, Netflix, and other non-essential expenses that enhance your lifestyle but aren't essential for your survival.
- **Designate 20% of your income for debt repayment and savings.** This section is essential so that you can pay down any outstanding debts, build up an emergency fund, and save up for future goals, like a home or retirement fund. It's crucial that you first take care of debt before considering saving up or investing. Also, always make sure to pay the highest-interest debt first.

The next priority is creating your emergency fund and only afterward, you can consider saving up for any of your goals and investing.

Your emergency fund is the first savings fund you should build before any other savings goals. A solid emergency fund should be about six-months' worth of mandatory expenses. This amount should give you enough of a financial safety net in case of job loss, illness, your car breaking down, or any other crisis scenario. This fund can vary based on individual life circumstances; single individuals are recommended to save six months of living expenses, while families with children or other dependents, like elder parents, should ideally set aside more, preferably nine to 12-months' worth of expenses.

When in doubt about how much you should allocate, it's better to err on the higher side of the recommendation. Needless to say, when used partially or fully, the emergency fund needs to be built back up before redirecting money to wants, savings, and investments.

The 50/30/20 "rule" should be regarded more as a guideline that helps provide a straightforward framework for money management, and, if necessary, adjustments can be made depending on individual circumstances. However, if you significantly stray away from these recommendations (for instance, the "needs" category takes up 90% of your income instead of 50%), it likely means that you cannot afford your lifestyle and should either look for ways to increase your income or decrease your lifestyle expenses.

To make your life easier when budgeting, use a spreadsheet or budgeting app—whichever suits your preferences better. I prefer apps since they're more easily available, as you have your phone handy at all times (unlike spreadsheets).

Another thing I've found useful is using a single card for my monthly expenses rather than spreading payments all over my accounts. Also, I don't use cash at all—I find it more efficient to pay for everything by card, as I can easily track in my bank app exactly how much I spent on everything, from groceries and bills to transportation, entertainment, and other expenses.

Remember, you don't need to navigate your financial journey alone—you can always ask your family or friends for guidance. Also, if you have a partner, ensure that you communicate openly with them about finances and work as a team to find solutions that work for both of you.

And if your ADHD makes managing finances particularly challenging, don't hesitate to seek assistance from a financial counselor, who can provide tailored guidance.

KEY TAKEAWAYS:

1. ADHD can make the entire process of money management feel daunting—executive challenges often translate into things

like misplacing financial documents, forgetting to pay bills, impulsive purchases, and overall poor money management.

2. While ADHD can make financial management tough, it doesn't mean that you can't achieve financial stability. Establishing routines and methods tailored to your ADHD strengths will help you manage your finances more effectively. Make sure to keep any systems and strategies streamlined, as you don't want their complexity to prevent you from using them long term.

3. Use the 50/30/20 framework for budgeting your money—allocate 50% of your income to your needs, 30% to your wants, and 20% to savings and investments. Before saving up or investing, make sure that you've paid off all your debt. Also, before working toward accomplishing any other savings goals, make sure to save up for an emergency fund, which should generally be equivalent to six-months' worth of non-discretionary expenses.

10

HOW TO MANAGE THE EMOTIONAL CHALLENGES OF ADHD

"Strength does not come from winning. Your struggles develop your strengths. When you go through hardships and decide not to surrender, that is strength."
— Gandhi

*I*f you've ever felt like your emotions have a mind of their own, swinging from sky-high ups to really low lows that no one else seems to experience, it's due to the emotional chaos that ADHD brings.

Many ADHDers face chronic struggles regulating their moods, handling criticism and rejection, and finding inner calm. This is also referred to as emotional dysregulation. In fact, over 70% of adults with ADHD encounter difficulties regulating their emotions (BioMed Central Psychiatry, 2020).

ADHD minds experience emotions rapidly and intensely. We can move quickly from calm to anger and from excitement to sadness, with little room for any in-betweens. We cycle between high-energy optimism and withdrawn, low motivation multiple times in a day as our attention and emotions fluctuate.

Our brains thrive on immediate gratification, leaving us little patience for delays, obstacles, or tedious tasks that prevent having our wants met quickly. We become emotionally frustrated when goals and rewards aren't instantly achievable.

We yearn for connection and approval from others, so even a hint of criticism hurts incredibly badly. We end up replaying negative scenarios over and over in our heads— dissecting how we've upset someone, for example—and every small rejection shakes the core of our self-worth.

The sour cherry on the cake is that due to our attention span challenges, we often struggle to identify and articulate all these intense emotions in a clear way. As a result, this makes it harder for others to empathize with us and offer the support we may need.

Causes of Emotional Dysregulation

Our different brain wiring is at the core of our emotional dysregulation. Brain imaging reveals that the limbic system, which has an essential role in regulating emotions, functions differently in ADHD brains. Our amygdala is more sensitive and quicker to activate, perceiving threats and triggering emotional reactions faster than a neurotypical amygdala would. It's like an overeager guard dog that reacts to the slightest noise.

Also, the prefrontal cortex in an ADHD brain has impaired connections to the limbic system, making it harder for us to engage in rational thinking before responding emotionally.

This results in a delay in applying "mental breaks" to pause and consider a thoughtful response. As a consequence, reactivity takes the forefront in our lives.

Moreover, the reduced availability of serotonin and dopamine in the ADHD brain contributes to mood instability—serotonin is responsible for regulating anxiety, happiness, and calmness, while dopamine influences motivation, reward seeking, and a sense of accomplishment. When these neurotransmitter levels dip, it destabilizes our emotional equilibrium.

A strong history of criticism can also play a significant role, as many of us were consistently corrected and shamed throughout the years for our forgetfulness, distraction, and disorganization. Not having an early diagnosis and being unaware that these were actually symptoms of a disorder and not personality traits led to internalized feelings of shame, as well as a strong fear of being judged as incapable or unintelligent. All this created increased rejection sensitivity and an overall guilt about who we are. Also, when ADHD is paired with another disorder, like anxiety or depression, it significantly worsens emotional dysregulation.

On top of that, fluctuating hormones, like estrogen and progesterone, during the menstrual cycle can further agitate emotional sensitivity. In the days leading up to your period when estrogen drops, it's common to experience worsening ADHD symptoms along with lower mood and irritability. Estrogen plays a role in dopamine availability, so when it declines during PMS week, dopamine also drops. This rollercoaster of shifting hormones on top of the baseline ADHD emotional reactivity creates the perfect storm for unstable moods.

ADHD-Related Emotional Difficulties & Relationships

The impact of ADHD-related emotional difficulties on our relationships can be profound. Our rapid, intense mood fluctuations often create a dynamic that others find perplexing and exhausting to navigate, putting strains on our bonds with romantic partners, friends, family, and colleagues.

There are moments when we feel overwhelmed by our emotions, causing us to snap at our loved ones. Paradoxically, on other occasions, we bottle up our feelings in order to avoid conflict, maintain peace, and avoid potential rejection.

Many of us with ADHD find ourselves trapped in the cycle of people pleasing, constantly trying to accommodate others' needs in the hope of gaining their approval. This strong desire for acceptance sometimes leads to such a strong fear of being negatively judged by others that we end up isolating ourselves socially as a protective measure. This fear stems from our heightened rejection sensitivity, causing us to perceive judgment or anger even when they're not present. For instance, in a situation where a friend appears to be quieter than usual, it may trigger our assumption that they're upset with us when, in reality, they may simply be tired or have other things on their mind. When we misread social cues, it further complicates our relationships.

Maintaining a proper balance of understanding and communication is needed from both sides. Navigating the complex emotional landscape of ADHD requires patience, empathy, and a shared commitment to fostering healthy connections.

Improving Self-Awareness

Cultivating a strong sense of self-awareness regarding the impact of ADHD on your emotions allows you to catch these patterns and improve your reactions over time. Below are some ways to start improving this essential virtue:

Pay attention to your emotions without judgment. When you notice a strong emotion, take a moment to pause and label it. Ask yourself, "What am I feeling right now?" Recognizing and acknowledging your emotions is the first step in effectively managing them. In addition, articulating the emotion with words makes the discomfort lose some of its power.

Learn your triggers. For one month, consistently keep a journal or use a note-taking app to track situations that regularly spark emotional reactions. Document the situations that caused intense feelings like anger, embarrassment, rejection, or hurt. Write in detail what happened right beforehand. Review these notes often and identify common triggers, focusing on whatever reactions frequently occur and what you want to address.

Notice signs of emotional escalation. Create a list of your typical physical indicators, such as headaches, tense muscles, sweaty palms, clenched fists, or nausea, which potentially indicate that you're starting to spiral emotionally. At the first body clue, pause and take a few deep breaths or go for a short walk to disrupt the escalation.

Track your mood fluctuations. This is easily done using a mood-tracking app like Daylio. Rate your mood daily on a scale of one to five (low to high energy) and note the factors impacting it. Review this data weekly and check for patterns. Are certain days or times consistently lower? What factors influence those dips? For example, PMS week is likely a potential common pattern among women with ADHD.

Understanding your patterns and triggers equips you with the knowledge that allows you to handle emotions intentionally instead of reactively. By spotting patterns and triggers as they're happening, you can quickly deploy strategies to self-soothe and de-escalate.

Behavioral Strategies

Aside from self-awareness, having go-to healthy outlets for managing emotions is essential for preventing getting stuck in negative cycles. You can detach from unhelpful thought patterns before falling down an anxiety spiral or anger tunnel. Learning a few strategies, like the ones below, can help you be proactive instead of reactive.

1. Mindfulness

Mindfulness is the practice of bringing full awareness and focus to the present moment rather than dwelling on the past or worrying about the future. Tuning into the present moment helps one detach from unhelpful thoughts.

For our busy ADHD minds that are prone to distraction, cultivating mindfulness is especially beneficial. Research[1] shows that it strengthens mental health by reducing anxiety, improving focus, and promoting overall emotional well-being. Some simple ways to incorporate it into your daily life:

- **Focused breathing:** This is one of the simplest yet most effective ways to practice mindfulness.

  - Find a quiet space, sit comfortably, and close your eyes.

- Take a deep breath through your nose, allowing your lungs to fill completely.
- As you exhale through your mouth, pay close attention to the sensation of the breath leaving your body. Focus fully on physical sensations, as well as sounds, sights, and smells around you without judgment whenever emotions intensify. Notice the air moving in and out.
- If your mind starts to wander, gently bring your focus back to your breath.

This exercise can be done for just a few minutes a day whenever you need help to stay grounded and centered.

- **Body scan meditation:** This exercise helps you become more in tune with your physical sensations, and it can be especially helpful for stress reduction and relaxation.

Start by lying down comfortably with your eyes closed. Bring awareness to different parts of your body, starting from your toes and working your way up to your head. As you focus on each body part, notice any sensations or tension without judgment. If you encounter tension, imagine sending your breath to that area, allowing it to relax.

- **Mindfulness while walking.** Engage in this practice by fully focusing on each step and feeling the ground beneath your feet. Pay attention to the sensation of the wind or sun against your face. Redirect your attention to walking if your thoughts wander.

If you're new to mindfulness and find it difficult to practice due to getting easily distracted, some guided meditations can help. There are various meditation apps as well as YouTube channels that offer free, guided mindfulness sessions. The structure and guidance make it easier for beginners to practice mindfulness effectively.

Start small with five to 10 minutes of daily mindfulness. Over time, you'll notice how it cultivates an ongoing sense of calmness and presence. Be patient with your mind when it wanders, and keep guiding it back with kindness. Observe your thoughts from a distance.

Remember, you are *not* your thoughts. Whenever you feel overwhelmed by your noisy brain, practice imagining your thoughts passing by like clouds. Acknowledge them, but don't latch on. Gently redirect your focus to the present moment by observing your surroundings or any sounds that you may hear in the moment.

2. Journaling

Write down your thoughts and feelings when experiencing emotional overwhelm. Putting pen to paper releases inner turmoil, and isn't that so much better than letting it bottle up?

After initially venting in a notepad or a piece of paper, try writing from a more rational, objective perspective. What kind of advice would you give to a friend in a similar situation?

Make journaling a daily habit, even for as little as 10 minutes. Remember—tracking patterns consistently will help you understand triggers.

3. Sensory Coping Techniques

- Listen to music and create playlists for different moods, like upbeat songs for motivation or peaceful acoustic for those moments when you struggle with anxiety.
- Get yourself a fidget toy so that you give your restless hands something to do and distract the mind.
- Use aromatherapy for emotional well-being, as essential oils can help with certain emotions. For

instance, lavender essential oil has a calming effect, lemon oil is energizing, and peppermint and rosemary oils have uplifting, focus-boosting benefits.

4. Self-Compassion

Be kind to yourself and acknowledge that everyone, whether living with ADHD or not, has emotional challenges. Understand that it's okay to have emotions and that you're actively working to manage them better! Below are some great strategies and philosophies to implement:

- Replace harsh self-talk with self-compassionate language. When you make a mistake or face a challenge, talk to yourself as you would to a close friend. Use kind, understanding, supportive words.

- Prioritize self-care activities that nourish your body and mind. These can include regular exercise, a balanced diet, sufficient sleep, relaxation techniques, or engaging in hobbies you enjoy. Self-care is a concrete way to demonstrate self-compassion.

- Set realistic expectations for yourself and don't hold yourself to unachievable standards. Recognize your limitations and set achievable goals, avoiding overcommitting or taking too much at once. Break goals into small, manageable ones, be patient with yourself, and celebrate your achievements always, no matter how big or small they are.

- Make sure to forgive yourself for past mistakes and imperfections. Remember that everyone makes them—they're part of our human nature! Also, these experiences are opportunities for growth and learning.

- Spend more time with supportive, understanding friends and family members who encourage self-compassion, and limit interactions with individuals who foster self-criticism or negativity.

Overall, be patient with yourself and approach this journey with kindness and understanding. Don't dwell on failure, but instead focus on what you can learn from it—analyze what went wrong and how you can apply those lessons in the future. When faced with setbacks, practice shifting your focus from dwelling on a problem to finding solutions and taking action to overcome challenges.

Besides these approaches, remember to consult your doctor about any potential medications that could help ease acute anxiety or emotional volatility if needed.

KEY TAKEAWAYS:

1. Over 70% of adults with ADHD encounter difficulties regulating their emotions.

2. The primary contributors to emotional dysregulation in ADHD brains include factors such as distinct brain wiring compared to neurotypical brains, reduced availability of serotonin and dopamine, a history of significant criticism, and fluctuating hormones.

3. ADHD-specific mood fluctuations can often create difficulties in our relationships with others.

4. Developing a strong sense of self-awareness is a crucial step in enhancing emotional management. Start by observing your emotions without judgment. Dedicate time to recognize any physical signs of emotional escalation. Keep a record of your mood fluctuations to discern patterns during specific triggering periods and situations.

5. Some behavioral strategies that can help you manage your emotions better include mindfulness practice, journaling, sensory coping techniques, and self-compassion.

FINAL THOUGHTS

"Most people are so preoccupied with the downside of the disorder that they fail to identify the gifts and talents that come along with it."
— Edward Hallowell, American psychologist and author

For too many years, women with ADHD have felt like misfits in a society that prioritizes conformity. We've long battled a harsh inner critic that constantly told us how forgetful, disorganized, lazy, and unfocused we were, labels that unfairly masked our true capabilities.

In a world that often seeks uniformity and order, ruled by the law of the majority, embracing our differences can be challenging. Yet, aren't these differences what make each of us special after all?

Perfection is an illusion. Aiming for "good enough" isn't a sign of failure but rather a recognition of your humanity. Accept that imperfections are part of each of us and our lives, and that they bring uniqueness and character to our journeys.

Don't compare yourself to others. Doing so is way too easy to do in a society like ours, and even more so now in the age of social media. Nobody should go through life thinking that they're not good enough. As the former American president Theodore Roosevelt said, "Comparison is the thief of joy."

Moreover, challenge any limiting beliefs you may have about what it means to have ADHD. Don't use your obstacles as a crutch to not strive for great achievements.

While ADHD is genetically influenced, genes alone don't determine outcomes and destinies. Your environment has a substantial influence and can be an extremely powerful mitigator of ADHD. You can't alter your DNA, but you can modify your lifestyle, eating, and sleeping habits, which can all have significant positive effects on your ADHD symptoms.

Seek out your people in ADHD communities, whether online or in person. Connect with those who walk a similar path and who can understand your experience. It's validating to share your challenges while also not having to worry about being judged.

If you feel safe with being vulnerable, open up to some of your close friends about your ADHD, as their support will mean the world. Send them articles to read, explain how your condition impacts you, and share what you need from them. Having one or two ride-or-die confidantes helps remind you you're not alone. We all need people who "get it" and who offer us empathy, validation, and accommodation. So make sure to surround yourself with people who both inspire you and sustain you during those difficult days.

Have a journal where you can write down your daily achievements, no matter how small they may seem. Cultivate the habit of acknowledging your successes, even the minor ones, and use this journal as a testament to your accomplishments and strengths. By redirecting focus toward achievement, you shift your attention away from imperfections and difficulties.

And, above all else, appreciate yourself for all that you are. Focus on those positive aspects of yourself that you appreciate and are grateful for. Show yourself grace and kindness and abandon self-judgment. *You are enough!*

ADHD is a journey of transformation, self-love, and celebration. There's a powerful liberation in understanding our neurological makeup and discovering the incredible potential lying dormant in our ADHD minds.

We deserve to acknowledge and honor all that we bring, not just the challenges. We spend so much time trying to "fix" our ADHD that we often overlook the special gifts that our neurotype brings.

Our differences are the source of incredible talents and skills. Let's acknowledge and always remember that without ADHD challenges, there would be no awesome ADHD qualities. Our minds are wired differently, sparking boundless imagination and original thinking. Our creativity manifests in various forms, whether it's developing ingenious solutions at work, producing beautiful art, or coming up with inventive recipes and DIY projects.

When we're passionate about a cause, hobby, or career, we approach it with an intensity that's both awe-inspiring and contagious. It's this very quality that allows us to turn our attention deficit around 180° and become hyper-focused when our passion is ignited. When we find something that intensely interests us, we can delve in for hours in an absorbed flow state and maintain a level of focus that's hard for neurotypicals to achieve. Our minds are incredibly curious, hungry for knowledge, and always looking for new things to learn and explore.

Our emotional sensitivity allows us to deeply empathize with how others are feeling, pushing us to offer a compassionate ear to those in need. We have the innate ability to tune into the subtle nuances of emotions, both in ourselves and in others. We have the skill of detecting unspoken emotions behind a smile or a frown. This is a quality that not only fosters profound connections but also contributes to our unique perspective on the human experience.

We're spontaneous and fun to be around. We're resilient and great in situations of crisis. I could go on and on about the many incredible qualities that make us who we are, but I'll stop here and allow you the space to explore within and recognize the many other positive aspects of your neurodiverse brain. Always remember the incredible qualities that ADHD brings!

As Thomas Armstrong, author of *The Power of Neurodiversity*, said in his book, *"Instead of pretending there is hidden away in a vault somewhere a perfectly 'normal' brain to which all other brains must be compared, we need to admit there is no standard brain, just as there is no standard flower or standard cultural or racial group, and that, in fact, diversity among brains is just as wonderfully enriching as biodiversity and the diversity among cultures and races."*

Finally, refer to this book often, as it'll continue to guide you on your path of releasing all your emotional baggage and embracing the unique strengths of your neurodiverse brain. With everything that's been outlined within these pages, you'll begin to recognize your positive ADHD qualities that have been there all along, hidden underneath the deficits that our society unfairly focuses on. You're now on your way to slowly rewriting your inner narrative and seeing neurodivergence as what it really is—a difference, not a defect.

THANK YOU!

Out of all the books out there, you chose to read this one... and for that, I'm incredibly grateful — thank you so much!

This book is a labor of love, and a lot of work went into it before it landed in your hands. So, if you feel like you gained any value from it, please take a moment to review it on the platform.

Your reviews will assist other women with ADHD in finding the information they're looking for and, as a solo indie author, enable me to continue writing more books and sharing more knowledge.

I read each and every review and would love to hear from you.

Much love,

Wilda

To leave your review simply scan the QR code below:

ENDNOTES

1. Adhd 101

1. Neurotransmitters are chemical messengers in the brain that transmit signals between nerve cells, influencing functions like mood, behavior and cognition.
2. DSM III and DSM IV are abbreviations referring to the third and fourth edition of the *Diagnostic and Statistical Manual of Mental Disorders*.
3. Executive function is an umbrella term referring to the mental processes that allow us to successfully focus, plan, organize, prioritize, remember instructions, and multitask. The neurotransmitter imbalances and structural differences of the ADHD brain impact our executive function skills.
4. Partners, C. (2016, September 7). ADHD in women. https://www.clinical-partners.co.uk/insights-and-news/item/adhd-in-women-why-is-it-so-undiagnosed#:~:text=But%20the%20fact%20is%20women,women%20with%20ADHD%20go%20undiagnosed.
5. Crawford, N. S. (2003, February). ADHD: a women's issue. https://www.apa.org/monitor/feb03/adhd
6. Ottosen, C., Larsen, J. T., Faraone, S. V., Chen, Q., Hartman, C. A., Larsson, H., Petersen, L., & Dalsgaard, S. (2019). Sex Differences in comorbidity Patterns of Attention-Deficit/Hyperactivity Disorder. *Journal of the American Academy of Child and Adolescent Psychiatry*, 58(4), 412-422.e3. https://doi.org/10.1016/j.jaac.2018.07.910

2. Conventional & Alternative Solutions for ADHD

1. Advokat, C., & Scheithauer, M. (2013). Attention-deficit hyperactivity disorder (ADHD) stimulant medications as cognitive enhancers. *Frontiers in Neuroscience*, 7. https://doi.org/10.3389/fnins.2013.00082

   Budur K, Mathews M, Adetunji B, Mathews M, Mahmud J. Non-stimulant treatment for attention deficit hyperactivity disorder. Psychiatry (Edgmont). 2005 Jul;2(7):44-8. PMID: 21152160; PMCID: PMC3000197.
2. He S, Wang M, Si J, Zhang T, Cui H, Gao X. Efficacy and safety of ginkgo preparations for attention deficit hyperactivity disorder: a systematic review protocol. BMJ Open. 2018 Feb 20;8(2):e020434. doi: 10.1136/bmjopen-2017-020434. PMID: 29463592; PMCID: PMC5855296.

3. Kim, H., Hong, J. T., & Park, M. H. (2015). Centella asiatica enhances neurogenesis and protects neuronal cells against H2O2-induced oxidative injury. Journal of Biomedical Research, 16(3), 121–128. https://doi.org/10.12729/jbr.2015.16.3.121

4. Lean protein refers to protein sources low in saturated fat

5. Dighriri IM, Alsubaie AM, Hakami FM, Hamithi DM, Alshekh MM, Khobrani FA, Dalak FE, Hakami AA, Alsueaadi EH, Alsaawi LS, Alshammari SF, Alqahtani AS, Alawi IA, Aljuaid AA, Tawhari MQ. Effects of Omega-3 Polyunsaturated Fatty Acids on Brain Functions: A Systematic Review. Cureus. 2022 Oct 9;14(10):e30091. doi: 10.7759/cureus.30091. PMID: 36381743; PMCID: PMC9641984.

6. Arnold LE, Lofthouse N, Hurt E. Artificial food colors and attention-deficit/hyperactivity symptoms: conclusions to dye for. Neurotherapeutics. 2012 Jul;9(3):599-609. doi: 10.1007/s13311-012-0133-x. PMID: 22864801; PMCID: PMC3441937.

Kemp A. Food additives and hyperactivity. BMJ. 2008 May 24;336(7654):1144. doi: 10.1136/bmj.39582.375336.BE. PMID: 18497374; PMCID: PMC2394588.

Kim Y, Chang H. Correlation between attention deficit hyperactivity disorder and sugar consumption, quality of diet, and dietary behavior in school children. Nutr Res Pract. 2011 Jun;5(3):236-45. doi: 10.4162/nrp.2011.5.3.236. Epub 2011 Jun 21. PMID: 21779528; PMCID: PMC3133757.

4. How to Navigate Executive Function Challenges

1. Diamond A. Executive functions. Annu Rev Psychol. 2013;64:135-68. doi: 10.1146/annurev-psych-113011-143750. Epub 2012 Sep 27. PMID: 23020641; PMCID: PMC4084861.

2. *Loci* in Latin means "locations."

5. How to Build Healthy, Long-Lasting Habits

1. Lally, P., Van Jaarsveld, C. H. M., Potts, H. W. W., & Wardle, J. (2009). How are habits formed: Modelling habit formation in the real world. European Journal of Social Psychology, 40(6), 998–1009. https://doi.org/10.1002/ejsp.674

10. How to Manage the Emotional Challenges of ADHD

1. Zylowska, L., Ackerman, D. L., Yang, M. H., Futrell, J. L., Horton, N. L., Hale, T. S., Pataki, C., & Smalley, S. L. (2008). Mindfulness Meditation Training in Adults and Adolescents With ADHD: A Feasibility Study. Journal of Attention Disorders, 11(6), 737-746. https://doi.org/10.1177/1087054707308502

OTHER BOOKS BY THE AUTHOR

BIBLIOGRAPHY

Adhikari, B. M., Bajracharya, A., & Shrestha, A. K. (2015). Comparison of nutritional properties of Stinging nettle (Urtica dioica) flour with wheat and barley flours. *Food Science and Nutrition*, *4*(1), 119–124. https://doi.org/10.1002/fsn3.259

Advokat, C., & Scheithauer, M. (2013). Attention-deficit hyperactivity disorder (ADHD) stimulant medications as cognitive enhancers. *Frontiers in Neuroscience*, *7*. https://doi.org/10.3389/fnins.2013.00082

Aguiar, S., & Borowski, T. (2013). Neuropharmacological Review of the Nootropic Herb Bacopa monnieri. *Rejuvenation Research*, *16*(4), 313–326. https://doi.org/10.1089/rej.2013.1431

Arnold, L. E., Lofthouse, N., & Hurt, E. (2012). Artificial Food Colors and Attention-Deficit/Hyperactivity Symptoms: Conclusions to Dye for. *Neurotherapeutics*, *9*(3), 599–609. https://doi.org/10.1007/s13311-012-0133-x

Bent, S., Padula, A., Moore, D. H., Patterson, M., & Mehling, W. (2006). Valerian for Sleep: A Systematic Review and Meta-Analysis. *The American Journal of Medicine*, *119*(12), 1005–1012. https://doi.org/10.1016/j.amjmed.2006.02.026

Bhusal, K. K., Magar, S. K., Thapa, R., Lamsal, A., Bhandari, S., Maharjan, R., Shrestha, S., & Shrestha, J. (2022). Nutritional and pharmacological importance of stinging nettle (Urtica dioica L.): A review. *Heliyon*, *8*(6), e09717. https://doi.org/10.1016/j.heliyon.2022.e09717

Budur, K., Mathews, M., Adetunji, B., & Mahmud, J. (2005, July 1). *Non-stimulant treatment for attention deficit hyperactivity disorder*. PubMed. https://pubmed.ncbi.nlm.nih.gov/21152160/

Ccc-Slp, L. a. Y. M. (2021, August 8). *Improve your working memory with 60 quick exercises*. EatSpeakThink.com. https://eatspeakthink.com/improve-working-memory-60-exercises/

Chandrasekhar, K., Kapoor, J., & Anishetty, S. (2012). A prospective, randomized Double-Blind, Placebo-Controlled study of safety and efficacy of a High-Concentration Full-Spectrum extract of ashwagandha root in reducing stress and anxiety in adults. *Indian Journal of Psychological Medicine*, *34*(3), 255–262. https://doi.org/10.4103/0253-7176.106022

Cicero, A. F. G., Derosa, G., Brillante, R., Bernardi, R., Nascetti, S., & Gaddi, A. V. (2004). EFFECTS OF SIBERIAN GINSENG (ELEUTHEROCOCCUS SENTICOSUS MAXIM.) ON ELDERLY QUALITY OF LIFE: a

RANDOMIZED CLINICAL TRIAL. *Archives of Gerontology and Geriatrics, 38,* 69–73. https://doi.org/10.1016/j.archger.2004.04.012

Complementary & Alternative Medicine for Mental Health. (2016, April 8). https://www.mhanational.org/. https://www.mhanational.org/sites/default/files/MHA_CAM.pdf

Coufal, L. (2023, August 31). *Decluttering with ADHD: tips for best results.* The Simple Daisy. https://thesimpledaisy.com/decluttering-with-adhd-tips-for-best-results/

Crawford, N. S. (2003, February). *ADHD: a women's issue.* https://www.apa.org. https://www.apa.org/monitor/feb03/adhd

Cummins, M. (2023, November 17). *ADHD and habits: What helps form them.* Marla Cummins. https://marlacummins.com/adhd-and-habits-making-them-stick/

Darbinyan, V., Kteyan, A., Panossian, A., Gabrielian, E., Wikman, G., & Wagner, H. (2000). Rhodiola rosea in stress induced fatigue — A double blind cross-over study of a standardized extract SHR-5 with a repeated low-dose regimen on the mental performance of healthy physicians during night duty. *Phytomedicine, 7*(5), 365–371. https://doi.org/10.1016/s0944-7113(00)80055-0

De Bock, K., Eijnde, B. O., Ramaekers, M., & Hespel, P. (2004). Acute Rhodiola rosea intake can improve endurance exercise performance. *International Journal of Sport Nutrition and Exercise Metabolism, 14*(3), 298–307. https://doi.org/10.1123/ijsnem.14.3.298

Diamond, A. (2013). Executive functions. *Annual Review of Psychology, 64*(1), 135–168. https://doi.org/10.1146/annurev-psych-113011-143750

Dighriri, I. M., Alsubaie, A. M., Hakami, F. M., Hamithi, D., Alshekh, M. M., Khobrani, F. A., Dalak, F. E., Hakami, A. A., Alsueaadi, E. H., Alsaawi, L. S., Alshammari, S. F., Alqahtani, A. S., Alawi, I. A., Aljuaid, A. A., & Tawhari, M. Q. (2022). Effects of omega-3 polyunsaturated fatty acids on brain functions: a systematic review. *Cureus.* https://doi.org/10.7759/cureus.30091

Eric. (2023, December 19). *ADHD diet for adults: Foods to eat and avoid.* ADDA - Attention Deficit Disorder Association. https://add.org/adhd-diet/

Gan, J., Galer, P. D., Ma, D., Chen, C., & Xiong, T. (2019). The Effect of Vitamin D Supplementation on Attention-Deficit/Hyperactivity Disorder: A Systematic Review and Meta-Analysis of Randomized Controlled Trials. *Journal of Child and Adolescent Psychopharmacology, 29*(9), 670–687. https://doi.org/10.1089/cap.2019.0059

Gertz, M., Zheng, Q., Xu, M., Zhou, X., Lü, L., Li, Z., & Zheng, G. (2018). Rhodiola rosea L. Improves Learning and Memory Function: Preclinical

Evidence and Possible Mechanisms. *Frontiers in Pharmacology, 9.* https://doi.org/10.3389/fphar.2018.01415

Ghazizadeh, J., Sadigh-Eteghad, S., Marx, W., Fakhari, A., Hamedeyazdan, S., Torbati, M., Taheri-Tarighi, S., Araj–Khodaei, M., & Mirghafourvand, M. (2021). The effects of lemon balm (Melissa officinalis L.) on depression and anxiety in clinical trials: A systematic review and meta-analysis. *Phytotherapy Research, 35*(12), 6690–6705. https://doi.org/10.1002/ptr.7252

Gonzáles, G. F. (2012). Ethnobiology and Ethnopharmacology ofLepidium meyenii(Maca), a Plant from the Peruvian Highlands. *Evidence-based Complementary and Alternative Medicine, 2012,* 1–10. https://doi.org/10.1155/2012/193496

Habit-Forming 101, Part 1: How to Build Habits with ADHD | Online anxiety therapy for anxious millennials. (n.d.). https://www.millennialtherapy.com/anxiety-therapy-blog/how-to-build-habits-with-adhd

He, S., Wang, M., Si, J., Zhang, T., Cui, H., & Gao, X. (2018). Efficacy and safety of ginkgo preparations for attention deficit hyperactivity disorder: a systematic review protocol. *BMJ Open, 8*(2), e020434. https://doi.org/10.1136/bmjopen-2017-020434

How the Gender Gap Leaves Girls and Women Undertreated for ADHD - CHADD. (2022, March 15). CHADD. https://chadd.org/adhd-news/adhd-news-adults/how-the-gender-gap-leaves-girls-and-women-undertreated-for-adhd/

Huang, D., Hu, Z., & Yu, Z. (2013). Eleutheroside B or E enhances learning and memory in experimentally aged rats. *PubMed.* https://doi.org/10.3969/j.issn.1673-5374.2013.12.005

Hussain, S. M., Farhana, S. A., Alshammari, M. S., Alnasser, S. M., Alenzi, N., Alanazi, S., & Nandakumar, K. (2022). Cognition enhancing effect of rosemary (Rosmarinus officinalis L.) in lab animal studies: a systematic review and meta-analysis. *Brazilian Journal of Medical and Biological Research, 55.* https://doi.org/10.1590/1414-431x2021e11593

Kasprzak, D., Jodłowska–Jędrych, B., Borowska, K., & Wójtowicz, A. (2018). Lepidium meyenii(Maca) – multidirectional health effects – review. *Current Issues in Pharmacy and Medical Sciences, 31*(3), 107–112. https://doi.org/10.1515/cipms-2018-0021

Kemp, A. (2008). Food additives and hyperactivity. *The BMJ, 336*(7654), 1144. https://doi.org/10.1136/bmj.39582.375336.be

Kennedy, D. O., Scholey, A., Tildesley, N. T. J., Perry, E. K., & Wesnes, K. (2002). Modulation of mood and cognitive performance following acute administration of Melissa officinalis (lemon balm). *Pharmacology, Biochemistry and Behavior, 72*(4), 953–964. https://doi.org/10.1016/s0091-3057(02)00777-3

Kim, H., Hong, J. T., & Park, M. H. (2015). Centella asiatica enhances neurogenesis and protects neuronal cells against H2O2-induced oxidative injury. *Journal of Biomedical Research*, *16*(3), 121–128. https://doi.org/10.12729/jbr.2015.16.3.121

Kim, Y., & Hyeja, C. (2011). Correlation between attention deficit hyperactivity disorder and sugar consumption, quality of diet, and dietary behavior in school children. *Nutrition Research and Practice*, *5*(3), 236. https://doi.org/10.4162/nrp.2011.5.3.236

Kongkeaw, C., Dilokthornsakul, P., Thanarangsarit, P., Limpeanchob, N., & Scholfield, C. N. (2014). Meta-analysis of randomized controlled trials on cognitive effects of Bacopa monnieri extract. *Journal of Ethnopharmacology*, *151*(1), 528–535. https://doi.org/10.1016/j.jep.2013.11.008

Lai, P., Naidu, M., Sabaratnam, V., Wong, K., David, R. P., Kuppusamy, U. R., Abdullah, N., & Malek, S. N. A. (2013). Neurotrophic Properties of the Lion's Mane Medicinal Mushroom, Hericium erinaceus (Higher Basidiomycetes) from Malaysia. *International Journal of Medicinal Mushrooms*, *15*(6), 539–554. https://doi.org/10.1615/intjmedmushr.v15.i6.30

Lally, P., Van Jaarsveld, C. H. M., Potts, H. W. W., & Wardle, J. (2009). How are habits formed: Modelling habit formation in the real world. *European Journal of Social Psychology*, *40*(6), 998–1009. https://doi.org/10.1002/ejsp.674

Landaas, E. T., Aarsland, T. I. M., Ulvik, A., Halmøy, A., Ueland, P. M., & Haavik, J. (2016). Vitamin levels in adults with ADHD. *British Journal of Psychiatry Open*, *2*(6), 377–384. https://doi.org/10.1192/bjpo.bp.116.003491

Lee, J., Lee, A., Kim, J., Shin, Y., Kim, S., Cho, W. D., & Lee, S. I. (2020). Effect of Omega-3 and Korean Red Ginseng on Children with Attention Deficit Hyperactivity Disorder: An Open-Label Pilot Study. *Clinical Psychopharmacology and Neuroscience: The Official Scientific Journal of the Korean College of Neuropsychopharmacology*, *18*(1), 75–80. https://doi.org/10.9758/cpn.2020.18.1.75

Lee, S. H., Park, W. S., & Lim, M. H. (2011). Clinical effects of Korean red ginseng on attention deficit hyperactivity disorder in children: an observational study. *Journal of Ginseng Research*, *35*(2), 226–234. https://doi.org/10.5142/jgr.2011.35.2.226

Li, I., Lee, L., Tsai-Teng, T., Chen, W., Chen, Y., Shiao, Y., & Chen, C. (2018). Neurohealth Properties ofHericium erinaceusMycelia Enriched with Erinacines. *Behavioural Neurology*, *2018*, 1–10. https://doi.org/10.1155/2018/5802634

Managing Money and ADHD - CHADD. (2019, February 27). CHADD. https://chadd.org/for-adults/managing-money-and-adhd/

Medication Management - CHADD. (2020, October 6). CHADD. https://chadd.org/for-adults/medication-management/

Memory, A. O. (2023, April 3). *How to build a memory Palace.* Art of Memory. https://artofmemory.com/blog/how-to-build-a-memory-palace/

Mirza, F. J., Amber, S., Sumera, S., Hassan, D., Ahmed, T., & Zahid, S. (2021). Rosmarinic acid and ursolic acid alleviate deficits in cognition, synaptic regulation and adult hippocampal neurogenesis in an Aβ1-42-induced mouse model of Alzheimer's disease. *Phytomedicine, 83,* 153490. https://doi.org/10.1016/j.phymed.2021.153490

Negative Self-Talk and How To Change It: ADHD Edition | Online Anxiety therapy for anxious Millennials. (n.d.). https://www.millennialtherapy.com/anxiety-therapy-blog/adhd-and-negative-thoughts

Nigg, J., PhD. (2023, November 6). *Epigenetics and ADHD: the impacts of environment, lifestyle, and stress.* ADDitude. https://www.additudemag.com/epigenetics-and-adhd-how-environment-impacts-symptoms/

Organizing the Home and Office Space - CHADD. (2019a, May 14). CHADD. https://chadd.org/for-adults/organizing-the-home-and-office-space/

Organizing the Home and Office Space - CHADD. (2019b, May 14). CHADD. https://chadd.org/for-adults/organizing-the-home-and-office-space/

Ottosen, C., Larsen, J. T., Faraone, S. V., Chen, Q., Hartman, C. A., Larsson, H., Petersen, L., & Dalsgaard, S. (2019). Sex Differences in comorbidity Patterns of Attention-Deficit/Hyperactivity Disorder. *Journal of the American Academy of Child and Adolescent Psychiatry, 58*(4), 412-422.e3. https://doi.org/10.1016/j.jaac.2018.07.910

Pacheco, D., & Pacheco, D. (2023, November 8). *Best temperature for sleep.* Sleep Foundation. https://www.sleepfoundation.org/bedroom-environment/best-temperature-for-sleep

Partners, C. (2016, September 7). *ADHD in women.* https://www.clinical-partners.co.uk/insights-and-news/item/adhd-in-women-why-is-it-so-undiagnosed

Pedersen, T. (2022, March 31). *Memory and mnemonic devices.* Psych Central. https://psychcentral.com/lib/memory-and-mnemonic-devices

Peth-Nui, T., Wattanathorn, J., Muchimapura, S., Tong-Un, T., Piyavhatkul, N., Rangseekajee, P., Ingkaninan, K., & Vittaya-Areekul, S. (2012). Effects of 12-WeekBacopa MonnieriConsumption on attention, cognitive processing, working memory, and functions of both cholinergic and monoaminergic systems in healthy elderly volunteers. *Evidence-based Complementary and Alternative Medicine, 2012,* 1–10. https://doi.org/10.1155/2012/606424

Potts, S. (2023, December 14). Executive Dysfunction & ADHD: The Relation, Signs & Treatments. *Beyond Book Smart.* https://www.beyondbooksmart.com/executive-functioning-strategies-blog/executive-dysfunction-101-how-to-treat-adhds-most-difficult-symptom

Professional, C. C. M. (n.d.). *Executive dysfunction.* Cleveland Clinic.

https://my.clevelandclinic.org/health/symptoms/23224-executive-dysfunction

Protein: What you need to know. (n.d.). *British Heart Foundation.* https://www.bhf.org.uk/informationsupport/heart-matters-magazine/nutrition/protein

Rabinovici, G. D., Stephens, M., & Possin, K. L. (2015). Executive dysfunction. *CONTINUUM: Lifelong Learning in Neurology,* 21, 646–659. https://doi.org/10.1212/01.con.0000466658.05156.54

Raghavan, A., & Shah, Z. A. (2014). Repair and regeneration properties of Ginkgo biloba after ischemic brain injury. *Neural Regeneration Research,* 9(11), 1104. https://doi.org/10.4103/1673-5374.135308

Rahbardar, M. G., & Hosseinzadeh, H. (2020). Therapeutic effects of rosemary (Rosmarinus officinalis L.) and its active constituents on nervous system disorders. *PubMed,* 23(9), 1100–1112. https://doi.org/10.22038/ijbms.2020.45269.10541

Roodenrys, S. (2002). Chronic Effects of Brahmi (Bacopa monnieri) on Human Memory. *Neuropsychopharmacology,* 27(2), 279–281. https://doi.org/10.1016/s0893-133x(01)00419-5

Rowe, S. (2021, July 7). *Neurotransmitters involved in ADHD.* Psych Central. https://psychcentral.com/adhd/neurotransmitters-involved-in-adhd#adhd-and-neurotransmitters

Sangiovanni, E., Brivio, P., Dell'Agli, M., & Calabrese, F. (2017). Botanicals as modulators of Neuroplasticity: Focus on BDNF. *Neural Plasticity,* 2017, 1–19. https://doi.org/10.1155/2017/5965371

Sari, D. C. R., Arfian, N., Tranggono, U., Setyaningsih, W. a. W., Romi, M. M., & Emoto, N. (2019). Centella asiatica (Gotu kola) ethanol extract up-regulates hippocampal brain-derived neurotrophic factor (BDNF), tyrosine kinase B (TrkB) and extracellular signal-regulated protein kinase 1/2 (ERK1/2) signaling in chronic electrical stress model in rats. *PubMed,* 22(10), 1218–1224. https://doi.org/10.22038/ijbms.2019.29012.7002

Scholey, A., Gibbs, A. A., Neale, C., Perry, N., Ossoukhova, A., Bilog, V., Kras, M., Scholz, C., Sass, M., & Buchwald–Werner, S. (2014). Anti-Stress effects of Lemon Balm-Containing foods. *Nutrients,* 6(11), 4805–4821. https://doi.org/10.3390/nu6114805

Shinjyo, N., Waddell, G., & Green, J. (2020). Valerian Root in Treating Sleep Problems and Associated Disorders—A Systematic Review and Meta-Analysis. *Journal of Evidence-Based Integrative Medicine,* 25, 2515690X2096732. https://doi.org/10.1177/2515690x20967323

Singh, N., Bhalla, M., De Jager, P., & Gîlcă, M. (2011). An overview on Ashwagandha: A rasayana (Rejuvenator) of Ayurveda. *African Journal of*

Traditional, Complementary and Alternative Medicines, *8*(5S). https://doi.org/10.4314/ajtcam.v8i5s.9

Stojcheva, E. I., & Quintela, J. C. (2022). The Effectiveness of Rhodiola rosea L. Preparations in Alleviating Various Aspects of Life-Stress Symptoms and Stress-Induced Conditions—Encouraging Clinical Evidence. *Molecules*, *27*(12), 3902. https://doi.org/10.3390/molecules27123902

Stough, C., Lloyd, J., Clarke, J., Downey, L. A., Hutchison, C., Rodgers, T., & Nathan, P. J. (2001). The chronic effects of an extract of Bacopa monniera (Brahmi) on cognitive function in healthy human subjects. *Psychopharmacology*, *156*(4), 481–484. https://doi.org/10.1007/s002130100815

Symptoms and diagnosis of ADHD | CDC. (2022, July 26). Centers for Disease Control and Prevention. https://www.cdc.gov/ncbddd/adhd/diagnosis.html

Thapar, A., & Stergiakouli, E. (2009). An overview on the genetics of ADHD. *Acta Psychologica Sinica*, *40*(10), 1088–1098. https://doi.org/10.3724/sp.j.1041.2008.01088

Thriving with ADHD. (2020, January 6). *Developing Social Competence - Thriving with ADHD*. Thriving With ADHD. https://thrivingwithadhd.com.au/developing-social-competence/

Watson, S. (2021, July 20). *Dopamine: The pathway to pleasure*. Harvard Health. https://www.health.harvard.edu/mind-and-mood/dopamine-the-pathway-to-pleasure#:~:text=Neurons%20in%20the%20region%20at,enzymes%20turn%20it%20into%20dopamine.

Website, N. (2023, March 13). *Symptoms*. nhs.uk. https://www.nhs.uk/conditions/attention-deficit-hyperactivity-disorder-adhd/symptoms/

Workplace issues - CHADD. (2022, October 19). CHADD. https://chadd.org/for-adults/workplace-issues/

Yamauchi, Y., Ge, Y., Yoshimatsu, K., Komatsu, K., Kuboyama, T., Yang, X., & Tohda, C. (2019). Memory Enhancement by Oral Administration of Extract of Eleutherococcus senticosus Leaves and Active Compounds Transferred in the Brain. *Nutrients*, *11*(5), 1142. https://doi.org/10.3390/nu11051142

Zylowska, L., Ackerman, D. L., Yang, M., Futrell, J. L., Horton, N. L., Hale, T. S., Pataki, C., & Smalley, S. L. (2007). Mindfulness meditation training in adults and adolescents with ADHD. *Journal of Attention Disorders*, *11*(6), 737–746. https://doi.org/10.1177/1087054707308502

Made in United States
Troutdale, OR
02/15/2024

17704469R00105